CORONA VICTUS

CORONA VICTUS

CONQUERING THE VIRUS OF FEAR

by Pastor Sam Polson

CORONA VICTUS
Written by Pastor Sam Polson

R.E.A.P. Guides by Joe Kappel
Edited by Lisa Soland

Text copyright © 2020 Sam Polson

CAUTION: All rights reserved. No part of this publication may be reproduced, stored in a retrieval system, or transmitted in any form or by any means electronic, mechanical, photocopy, recording, or other, except for brief quotations in written reviews, without the prior written permission of the publisher.

Most Scripture quotations are from the ESV® Bible (The Holy Bible, English Standard Version®), copyright © 2001 by Crossway, a publishing ministry of Good News Publishers. Used by permission. All rights reserved.

Published in 2020 by:
Climbing Angel Publishing
PO Box 32381
Knoxville, Tennessee 37930
http://www.ClimbingAngel.com

First Edition: July 2020
Printed in the United States of America
Cover design by PrintEdge
Author photo by Stefan Holt
Interior design by Climbing Angel Publishing

ISBN: 978-1-64921-803-2
Library of Congress Control Number: 2020909635

This book is lovingly dedicated
to my sister-in-law, Carol Bittner,
who won her Victor's Crown
April 6, 2020

Contents

Foreword — xi

Introduction — xiii

R.E.A.P. — xvii

1 - The Prince at Peace — 1

2 - The Focus of Faith — 15

3 - Is Good Friday, Good? — 31

4 - The Conqueror of Death — 43

5 - The Vaccine for Fear — 57

6 - The Therapy for Peace — 79

7 - The Guardians of the Mind — 97

8 - Sheltered in God — 115

Foreword

"To every thing there is a season, and a time to every purpose under the heaven" (Ecc. 3:1, NKJV). On this side of heaven, we may not always understand the purpose but we can know the season.

Twenty years ago I was blessed to enter into a special "season" of friendship with Pastor Sam Polson. I fondly remember the day my son, Samuel-David, was born. Within the hour, Pastor Sam showed up at the hospital, took my son into his arms, pressed him against his yellow sweater, and prayed a blessing over him. Without a doubt, the prayer blessed my son but witnessing that love and tenderness blessed me beyond measure as well. But the icing on the cake was this—ever since that day Pastor Sam has never once forgotten my son's birthday. He is always mindful to ask what my son is reading, how he's doing and leaves by saying, "Is there anything he needs?" I only share this because my son is not the only one who receives such love and steadfastness. I have heard countless young men and women, who are now serving as missionaries or pastors, reveal stories of the same type of caring connection to Pastor Sam.

Pastor Sam and I discovered true friendship similar to that described by Winnie the Pooh: "A day without a friend is like a pot without a single drop of honey left inside." Or better yet, "One who has unreliable friends soon comes to ruin, but there is a friend who sticks closer than a brother" (Pro. 18:24, NIV). I have been honored to journey through life with more than enough sweetness and faithfulness in this special season with my friend, Pastor Sam.

In today's society we have many preachers but what we long for are true, loving, *biblical shepherds*. Pastor Sam is one of those rare, loving, biblical shepherds as revealed daily by the fruit of his life. Every person also longs for *God's Word* as an anchor to pause, breathe, reflect, and meditate on. In Pastor Sam's new book, *Corona Victus*, you get both—a loving biblical shepherd gently sharing the truth of *God's Word*. Read this book and you will be reminded of God's victorious crown of life, providing every one of us with lasting freedom from fear.

I have read and reread *Corona Victus* and I know it will comfort you by making spiritual deposits of our most holy faith into your soul's depleted account due to the fearful withdrawals made via this COVID-19 pandemic. "R.E.A.P." this little book and it will read and transform you.

Corona Victus can be used for becoming victorious over a season of fear, but this book can also be used for every other season in your life. I'll be using it for family worship and hospital visits. I also plan to purchase extra copies to leave with the clients that I counsel.

In short, this little book has become one of my new friends. Ralph Waldo Emerson said, "A friend is a person with whom I may be sincere. Before him I may think aloud. I am arrived at last in the presence of a man so real and equal, that I may drop even those undermost garments of dissimulation, courtesy, and second thought, which men never put off, and may deal with him with the simplicity and wholeness with which one chemical atom meets another." And with regard to Sam Polson and his new book *Corona Victus*, I could not agree more.

Dr. David Trempe
Executive Chaplain, Royal Chaplain Corps
May 2020
Knoxville, TN

INTRODUCTION

I was traveling to a mission board meeting in another state when all the federal guidelines to implement "social distancing" were first announced to the nation. Our elders and staff immediately had to make plans via "social networking" to prepare for the coming Sunday gathering, without actually being able to gather. I certainly found it incredibly strange when Sunday arrived to be sitting at a desk in a hotel room watching the first live stream broadcast of a worship service taking place in the church that I pastor. All of it was going on without me being there! But I was also blessed to experience, along with my congregation, true *spiritual connecting* even as we gathered by means of the internet in a season of *"social distancing."* I was deeply encouraged to sense that what binds us together as God's people crosses all boundaries of location or isolation.

So often, our Lord uses the challenging experiences in our lives to provide deeper experiences with him. It is my sincere hope that this book will be used by our Heavenly Father to bring peace to your soul at times when it seems as if every landmark in your life is being shaken, or even obliterated. It is only natural that in such seasons we experience the very natural emotion of fear. However, there exists a power that can be truly felt in the deepest regions of our soul that is much more powerful and much more real than fear, and that is God's peace. His is a peace that truly surpasses all understanding and that guards our hearts and minds by the power of Jesus Christ himself. (Philippians 4:7) Fear is powerful, like a dreaded virus to our souls, but it is not ALL powerful. That power which reigns over all others is the power of the One who wears the

Victor's crown, the *Corona Victus*. My prayer for you today is that Jesus' victory will be your victory in *Conquering the Virus of Fear*.

Sam Polson
May 2020
Knoxville, TN

How to R.E.A.P.
the Word of God

Read: Read the passage carefully and prayerfully.

Examine: Read the passage again, noting keywords or phrases. Be careful to note the context surrounding the passage. Ask questions about the passage. Who is the audience? What situation is the speaker or author addressing? What is the main theme of this passage? Note in particular what you learn about the Lord from the passage.

Apply: Consider carefully the impressions on your heart as you read. How does this passage touch on specific areas or situations in your life? What wisdom are you gaining from this passage? What are you learning about your Lord in relation to your current spiritual experience?

Pray: Use what the Lord has revealed about Himself or about you personally in this time as an opportunity to respond directly to Him. Pray to Him in praise, or repentance, or in petition for others as the Holy Spirit guides you. Treat this time in God's Word not as a devotional exercise, but as a personal encounter with your holy God and your loving Savior.

- 1 -

THE PRINCE AT PEACE

On that day, when evening had come, he said to them, "Let us go across to the other side." And leaving the crowd, they took him with them in the boat, just as he was. And other boats were with him. And a great windstorm arose, and the waves were breaking into the boat, so that the boat was already filling. But he was in the stern, asleep on the cushion. And they woke him and said to him, "Teacher, do you not care that we are perishing?" And he awoke and rebuked the wind and said to the sea, "Peace! Be still!" And the wind ceased, and there was a great calm. He said to them, "Why are you so afraid? Have you still no faith?" And they were filled with great fear and said to one

another, "Who then is this, that even the wind and the sea obey him?"
(Mark 4:35-41)

Coronavirus.

I'm sure very few of us had ever heard of the word. Now we know the word all too well. It has become a word that we will, no matter how long we live, never forget again. Coronavirus is a word that has very quickly changed everything. Our life now is different, really different. And yes, at times it's a little scary because everything has been changed by this virus.

The coronavirus is something we cannot see. It is something we cannot really control. It is something that threatens our safety. It is a virus that has not only infected our communities but our country and our world. It is also infecting some of our fellow citizens. Our prayers are certainly with those who are sick with this virus and with those who have lost loved ones through the impact of this disease. The coronavirus brought many aspects of life, as we have known it for so long, to its knees. To put it plainly—this virus has rocked our world.

It's called the coronavirus because underneath the microscope the virus molecule looks like a crown. And right now, it seems like the coronavirus is ruling everything. It seems as if this virus is in control. But it isn't. It is not ruling anything at all. As believers, we know who wears the crown of the universe and that is the One who was crowned with thorns —the Lord Jesus Christ. He is King of kings and Lord of lords, and it is he who wears the crown.

It is on that changeless truth of Christ's lordship that I want to place our focus throughout the pages of this book. In a season when our senses are constantly being bombarded by the subject of *coronavirus*, we need to refocus our attention on *Corona Victus* because the victory has already been won by our

Lord Jesus Christ, and he shares this victory with those who trust in him. It is a victory over the virus of fear. It is the victory of faith. For "this is the victory that has overcome the world—our faith" (1 John 5:4). The Bible also says "we are more than conquerors through him who loved us" (Romans 8:37). That victory is not ancient history; it is the living reality of life in Jesus. In these two verses and many others, the writers of Scripture challenge us to *be who we are* and to *live what is ours* as conquerors in Christ. This victory includes the victory over the menacing virus of fear.

So, what does that look like? How should we respond in times like this? Of course, we face many limitations but the question remains: how should we respond to the deadly and highly infectious virus of fear?

As I mentioned earlier, when all of the implementations of social distancing began, I was attending a mission board meeting. On the opening morning of the sessions, I realized I had forgotten something in my car and headed to the parking lot to retrieve it. As I was going down the back stairs, I met a friend coming up. Harry is a missionary physician and a wonderful and talented follower of the Lord. We warmly greeted each other and then, of course, our conversation quickly landed on how we were dealing with the impact of the coronavirus pandemic.

Harry said, "Hey, let me read to you an email that someone just sent me. It's a quote in a letter from Martin Luther as Germany, in the 16th century, was visited by an outbreak of the bubonic plague." My friend continued to explain that Martin Luther was asked how he was going to respond to the virus and here is what Luther wrote back to his friend.

> *"I shall ask God mercifully to protect us. Then I shall fumigate, help purify the air, administer medicine, and take it. I shall avoid places and persons where my presence is not needed in order not to become*

contaminated and thus perchance infect and pollute others, and so cause their death as a result of my negligence. If God should wish to take me, he will surely find me and I have done what he has expected of me and so I am not responsible for either my own death or the death of others. If my neighbor needs me, however, I shall not avoid place or person but will go freely, as stated above. See, this is such a God-fearing faith because it is neither brash nor foolhardy and does not tempt God."
(Martin Luther, *Luther's Works*, Vol. 43: *Devotional Writings II*, ed. Jaroslav Jan Pelikan, Hilton C. Oswald, and Helmut T. Lehmann, vol. 43 (Philadelphia: Fortress Press, 1999), 119–38.

What a great statement with a great message for us. Although it was written 500 years ago, it is so timeless and timely in its application to us facing the current pandemic. So again we ask the question: what should be our faith response during frightening times like this when we are being tossed about in a very real storm of fear and the unknown?

In Mark 4:35-41, we have a recorded storm story, not from the weather channel but the Word of God. This story from the life of Jesus teaches us how we can keep our bearings by keeping a faith focus during the storms of life. We find in this passage of Scripture, four truths on which to focus during our stormy times.

1. THE PROVIDENCE OF GOD

The word providence means "control" or "guidance." The doctrine of God's providence undergirds everything we believe. In fact, all of life itself is supported by this truth of God's sovereign providence.

Divine providence means that this universe is not governed by randomness. The universe in which we live and have our being is guided by rationality and intentionality that comes from God himself.

In general application, Divine providence means that God, our Lord, permits all that happens. That is true, but we need to be careful here. God *is not* the author of sin. "God is light, and in him is no darkness at all" (1 John 1:5).

God is not the author of sin therefore he is not the author of the consequences of sin, which is the curse of sin on the world in which we live. And the curse of sin is in all of us as fallen image-bearers. God is not the author of sin yet God, in his divine providence, permits sin and sin's consequences to continue for a season. It is difficult to fully comprehend that providence means our Lord God permits all that happens.

I vividly remember Sunday, September 16, 2001. The churches were not empty; they were overflowing because of a national crisis that took place on Tuesday, September 11, or as we know it—9/11. I recall on that weekend being contacted by a local television station and asked if I would do a live interview Sunday at 6:30 am. When the segment began on live television, the first question the reporter asked me was, "So, Reverend Polson, why did God allow this to happen?"

My first thought was, "6:30 in the morning and you're asking me that kind of question?!" But inside my mind, I quickly prayed, then provided the reporter with the answer. (And I believe it was a biblical answer.) I said simply, "I don't know. And neither does anyone else." The truth is we don't know the answer to some things. They lie within the realm of Divine providence and only God knows.

One of the most important verses in the Word of God on this subject, which I believe will undergird your life and faith is Deuteronomy 29:29:

> The secret things belong to the Lord our God, but the things that are revealed belong to us and to our children forever, that we may do all the words of this law.

Now, notice in that verse this phrase: "The secret things belong to the Lord our God..." We do not know his plans for the things that he has not revealed. We cannot understand his mind. We don't know those things but the things that he has revealed are ours to receive and to believe and to pass on to our children. Divine providence does not mean, however, that life is a cosmic chess game with people as the pawns on God's chessboard. There is a gracious application of God's divine providence at work, which means our Lord has a plan for all things that happen to his people, and it is a gracious plan.

This story in Mark, Chapter 4 is a perfect illustration of Divine providence. The storm rocked all the boats that were out in the sea that day, but the Lord had a specific plan for his followers who were in one particular boat. It is very important to recognize that the disciples were not in this boat and in this storm because they were *out of the will of God*. They were in this boat and in this storm because they were *in the will of God*. The Lord Jesus Christ himself led his disciples into this boat and allowed them to sail into this storm. Their journey that day was a gracious plan of the Lord who loved them.

Now, when this storm swept over the disciples, Romans 8:28 had not yet been written by the inspired quill of the Apostle Paul. But what Paul wrote at a later date communicated an eternal truth:

> And we know that for those who love God all things work together for good, for those who are called according to his purpose. (Rom. 8:28)

Consider that verse. I mean, *really* look at that verse. Do you believe, *really* believe, that this statement is true?

Whether in a time of "social distancing," or in a time of physical or emotional or financial distressing, that promise of God's is still true. "And we know that for those who love God all things work together for good, for those who are called according to his purpose." Perhaps, my friend, where you are right now, you need to get really honest with Jesus by saying, Lord, "I believe; help my unbelief!" (Mark 9:24) It is the honest cry of a struggling heart. "I don't understand this; I can't wrap my mind around it because 'the secret things' belong to you, Lord. But this promise of Romans 8:28 has been revealed by you, and it is for me. I know this. Now, Lord God, please help me to take hold of this and believe it. Help me to believe in you during the storms of life, even this storm occurring in my life right now."

2. *PEACE OF OUR LORD*

We can shelter through any storm in the providence of our Lord Jesus Christ. But *how* do we do that? How do we shelter ourselves in the providence of our gracious Lord? By focusing on something else. We focus on *someone* else. We focus on the peace of our Lord!

Let's look at the two incredible contrasts going on in this boat. On the one hand, you have the disciples who are struggling and yelling and bailing out water for all they're worth. And now let's look at Jesus—sweetly napping in the stern of the boat without a wrinkle on his brow. He is surely the *Prince at peace*.

These disciples are made of the same human stuff we are made of now, and they are filled with fear. Jesus is in a quiet peace in the midst of their storm. He is resting peacefully and this incredibly frustrates the disciples. Their fear becomes frustration with their Lord who seems to be resting so comfortably while they are at such risk. That is the reason we are told in Mark 4:38 that they exclaimed, "Teacher, do you not care that we are perishing?" *How can you sleep so serenely while we are about to die here?!*

That question has been asked untold billions of times over the centuries. "Lord, do you not care that we are perishing?!" I wonder how many times in the last few months that cry has gone up from the people of God? There is a reality communicated here that we need to be honest about. Storms can cause us to *forget*. Storms can cause us to forget important things very quickly. We have this very human tendency, which is part of our fallenness, to forget in the storms what we learned in the calm. We have a tendency to forget in the darkness what we learned in the light.

We forget in the darkness what we learned in the light.

What is it that these disciples have forgotten? They have forgotten *who is onboard the boat*. They have forgotten *who is in the boat with them*. And in the providence of God, they are about to be reminded. This is God's *gracious* providence. This storm is a gracious gift to them, as they are going to be reminded of an incredible truth they will never forget for the rest of their lives. They are going to be reminded of the *power of the Lord*.

3. THE POWER OF THE LORD

Mark 4:39 tells us, "And he awoke and rebuked the wind and said to the sea, 'Peace! Be still!' And the wind ceased, and there was a great calm." The fearful storm that threatened to flood and sink the boat was subdued at the words of Jesus. This display of power caused another flood, a flood of fear that entered the hearts of these disciples. It was a different kind of fear than the fear of the storm. The awe-filled fear was expressed this way in verse 41, "Who then is this, that even the wind and the sea obey him?" They were speechless. *Who can this be that is in this boat with us, that the very wind and sea must obey?* The disciples were speechless but Jesus was not. It was now his turn to speak and their turn to listen. It was his turn to ask them a very probing question.

In Mark 4:40, Jesus asked them, "Why are you so afraid? Have you still no faith?" The one who had just rebuked the wind and the waves now rebukes their weakness—the weakness of their faith. You see, fear had made them faithless. They had allowed their fear to lead them to faithlessness. How did that happen? How did fear take away their faith? It took their faith away because their focus shifted. Fear had changed their focus. In their fear, their focus became fixated *on the disaster* that was threatening them, rather than *the master* who is with them.

In their fear, they forgot who was with them.

I want to tell you, shipmate, fear makes us forget who is on board in our lives. The old gospel song "Master, the Tempest Is Raging," written by Mary Ann Baker, shares our struggle:

> *Master, the tempest is raging*
> *Oh, The billows are tossing high*
> *The sky is o'ershadowed with blackness*
> *Oh, No shelter or help is nigh*
> *Carest thou not that we perish?*
> *How canst thou lie asleep*
> *When each moment so madly is threatning*
> *A grave in the angry deep?*

Fear makes us forget the truth. And what is the truth? It is the same truth that this same gospel song by Mary Ann Baker shares:

> *Whether the wrath of the storm-tossed sea*
> *Or demons or men or whatever it be,*
> *No waters can swallow the ship where lies*
> *The Master of ocean and earth and skies.*

That is the truth and we cannot let ourselves forget this truth in the midst of fear.

Jesus' challenge to his disciples about their fear was a challenge to faith. Where was their object of faith? Their object of faith rested in Jesus. It was not faith in their faith. It was not faith in their circumstances, certainly. But their faith that he challenged was their faith in him. In effect what Jesus is challenging them to remember is to *remember him*. My friend, that is how we stay in faith and keep walking in faith. That is how we overcome fear—when our focus remains on him, the Master of ocean and earth and sky. The master is in the boat. Our master is in *our* boat. He is our Prince and he is at peace. He is in the boat with us.

What is Jesus saying through this timely story? He is saying to his followers through the ages, to us as his people in this very fearful time in which we live right now, "Remember me in this storm. Focus on me in this storm, and you will have faith."

4. THE PRESENCE OF THE LORD

This is our challenge today—to remember the presence of the Lord. And that is the fourth focus in these gospel verses. The Lord never promised that we would not go through storms. In fact, the truth is just the opposite. Jesus said, "In the world you will have tribulation. But take heart; I have overcome the world" (John 16:33). Jesus did not promise that we would not go through storms. What he did promise was that we would never go through a single storm alone.

He promised, "And behold, I am with you always, to the end of the age" (Matt. 28:20). Jesus shared this just before he ascended into heaven. *No matter what comes, don't forget—I am with you always. Always!*

Dear friend, a Christian can be many things, but one thing he or she can never be is *alone*. Never. Ever. Today, the Lord is in your boat because he is in your heart if you are a Christian. He is in you. Christ in you—the hope of glory. So, in any circumstance or situation that you are in, whatever it may be—

you are not alone because Jesus is not just with you he is *within you*. The Lord Jesus Christ himself, by his Spirit, is in your heart right now.

I want to challenge you to declare this at this very moment. Just say it out loud. "He is with me." Or better still, if you are gathered as a family or as a couple, sharing this book together in Bible study, right now simply declare this together, "He is with us." If you don't know that Christ is in you, then know this—the storm of the coronavirus is nothing compared to the storm of the wrath of God that awaits those who reject his Son the Lord Jesus.

If you don't have that peace in your heart today, if you don't know that the Master of ocean and earth and sky is in your heart, that he is your very life, and he lives within you, then I beg you right now, wherever you are, kneel before the maker of heaven and earth, the Lord Jesus Christ. Call upon him in faith and ask him to forgive your sins. Trust him as your Lord and Savior. Surrender your life to him and he will speak his peace into your heart—the peace that surpasses all understanding—the peace of his salvation. He will say to you, "Peace, be still."

I pray that through this time of providence, you will be led to see that there is only one unchanging certainty and absolute safety, and that is in Jesus Christ our Lord. To know him and to have him as your Savior is to know peace. I pray that this will be your experience this very hour. And that God will confirm this truth in your heart by his Spirit. I pray that the Lord speak into your storm right now, just as he spoke into the storm with his disciples that day, "Peace, be still."

PRAYER

Almighty God and heavenly Father, we thank you that you are Infinite God. You are infinite in your glory, majesty, and mercy, for you are merciful to all who call upon you. You are full of kindness and compassion. Lord God, we pray that you will make us vessels of that compassion in ministry as we have opportunity. We thank you for your peace. We pray that your peace will reign, right now, in our hearts and lives. We pray that your peace will come to those who are trusting in you, surrendering to you as Lord and Savior.

O, Lord God, we pray that you will grant mercy to our country and this world. We pray that very soon, by your power, you will remove the scourge of this pestilence. Bless and strengthen all who are serving you by serving their fellow man. Give wisdom and insight to all who labor over and labor about this virus. We pray that you will keep our eyes focused on you, and remind us that you are not far away but with us in our every circumstance. We are not alone. We praise you for this and give you glory.

Amen.

R.E.A.P. GUIDE

READ
- Mark 4:35-41.
- What do you think the Holy Spirit intends to teach us from this passage?

EXAMINE
- What is the time of day when this account happens (35)?
- The storm that came on Jesus and the disciples was sudden; there is no way the disciples could have planned around it. How is the storm described? How did the disciples react during the storm?
- When they woke Jesus, what did he immediately do? What happened to the storm?
- Jesus rebuked the disciples for what reason?
- In the end, the disciples no longer fear the storm. What do they fear now, and why?

APPLY
- In what ways have you been tempted to fear during this time of the coronavirus?
- During times of fear, how do you identify with the disciples who doubted the Lord's care for them?
- What have you learned about the Lord Jesus from this account that will help you conquer fear?

PRAY
- Using the "PRAY" acronym, respond with **P**raise to the Lord, **R**epent of sins this Bible passage has revealed to you, **A**sk the Lord for any requests you have, and **Y**ield to his will.

- 2 -

The Focus of Faith

"Therefore, since we are surrounded by so great a cloud of witnesses, let us also lay aside every weight, and sin which clings so closely, and let us run with endurance the race that is set before us, looking to Jesus, the founder and perfecter of our faith, who for the joy that was set before him endured the cross, despising the shame, and is seated at the right hand of the throne of God."
(Heb. 12:1-2)

I shared in the introduction what an unusual experience it was for me to be out-of-town and watching the first live-streaming worship service at my own church that first Sunday after the establishment of the national "social distancing" guidelines. It occurred to me then that *no one* was actually sitting in the auditorium. All the congregants were watching the service online just like me. That was different, for sure. But that unusual moment was far surpassed the following Sunday when the most *surreal moment* I have ever had in ministry took place.

On that beautiful morning, I pulled into the West Park Baptist parking lot at about 9:25, and there before me were a grand total of four vehicles. Usually, at that time, there would be hundreds of cars parked there. I then entered the auditorium and found it *empty;* only a handful of people were there, preparing to lead the online worship service. An empty auditorium on Sunday morning! A pastor's nightmare! Eventually, two other men sat with me, using appropriate "social distancing," and as our worship pastor and small praise team led in songs of worship, the three of us joined in with all of our hearts. Our voices created quite a unique blend. I'm sure there is not an auditorium anywhere that we could not empty! Delivering the sermon, I gave it my very best to share the message in a personal and engaging way, although I was speaking to an empty auditorium. I spoke into a camera *I could not see*, and to an audience *that was not visible*. Other than that, it was a pretty typical preaching experience.

But it was actually *following* the service when I experienced the *most surreal moment* in my entire ministry. At about 11:45, I walked through the buildings on the campus of our church, on a Sunday morning, and they were completely empty. Usually, there are crowds in every hallway—children and adults running about—but now all the space was completely empty. I walked through the welcome center—empty. I came back into the auditorium—empty. But most of all, my heart was empty. And that is when it happened. The Spirit of the Lord clearly spoke to my heart. I deeply sensed him saying to me, "See this, Sam. *See this!*" And here is what I saw. In an *empty church building*, I saw *the church body*. It was perhaps the greatest reminder of my life that the church is not brick-and-mortar, nor is it a building. The actual church is a body, the body of Christ, and that morning *we had gathered* as that body just as sure as if we had met together physically. But more than that, millions of our brothers and sisters in Christ, all over the world, were gathering together that Sunday, even though their buildings were empty as well. That was a great moment for me. I understood that the body of Christ *was* together, gathering in Spirit and in Truth. God so encouraged me by allowing me to *see the invisible*.

Sometimes the Lord Jesus Christ takes our trials and makes them into our greatest triumphs. Certainly, we all experience intense times of trial, but these can become times of triumph through our Lord.

In the previous chapter, we discussed the Lord's providence, and we learned that *God in his providence allows us to experience trials so that we can learn to view the invisible and to value the invaluable*. It is in times of trial that the Lord helps us to *truly see* the invisible so we can more *value* what is invaluable.

We considered this truth in Chapter 1 as we read the story recorded in the Gospel of Mark, Chapter 4 of the disciples in the boat during a terrible storm. The boat was about to sink, but Jesus was sound asleep, taking a nap in the stern of the boat. In a frantic state, the disciples woke him asking, "Master, don't you care that we are perishing?" Jesus stood and rebuked the wind and the waves, and a calm came over the sea. Then, the awe-struck disciples asked themselves, "Who is this that even the winds and the seas obey him?" Do you remember the question Jesus asked them? He asked, "Why are you so afraid? Do you still have no faith?" Notice, Jesus connected the fullness of fear with a *failure of faith*. The fullness of fear that had controlled his disciples was really the result of a *failure of faith*. What did Jesus want his disciples to see in this storm?

Jesus wanted the disciples to see *him*.

Jesus was asleep in their boat. He was their Prince at peace. And if the Prince is at peace, his people do not have to be overcome with fear. Friends, Jesus is always in our boat. He was the disciples' peace over 2000 years ago, and he is our peace today. It is in seeing him that our faith is created, and it is in seeing Jesus that our faith is also sustained. The keyword is "seeing."

Faith must have a focus.

If we look *within ourselves* we will not find much cause for faith there. If we focus on what is going on around us, we won't find much there to bring faith either. But if we fix our eyes on Jesus, that is where faith is both created and sustained. Let's reflect on the passage that communicates this truth so beautifully—Hebrews 11. Notice what the writer of Hebrews reveals to us about faith.

WHAT IS FAITH?

The Book of Hebrews is a challenge for professing believers in the Messiah. In reading this scripture, we are challenged to persevere through difficult times by the power of faith. The author is speaking to believers who were going through terrible times of trial. The challenge is, "Don't turn back to unbelief; press on in faith." So we must ask the question again, "What is faith?" In Hebrews, Chapter 11, verses 1-2, the author shares with us the essence of faith:

> Now faith is the assurance of things hoped for, the conviction of things not seen. For by it the people of old received their commendation.

To make sure we truly understand faith, the writer of Hebrews gives us some wonderful *examples* of faith. Beginning at verse 7 through verse 40, we are provided examples of famous, infamous, and even unknown followers of God through the centuries. They are radically different in character and experience, yet they are all united by the one common denominator of faith.

We must remember that there were no chapter divisions in the original text of Scripture, so even though we move from Chapter 11 to Chapter 12, the theme of the writer's thoughts regarding faith continues. He defines the *essence* of faith and then describes several *examples* of faith. As Chapter 12 begins, the author shares with us what faith looks like and how it is expressed.

WHAT DOES FAITH LOOK LIKE?

If we are supposed to be people of faith, what does this expression of this faith look like? There is a simple but profound answer, so please don't miss this—faith looks a lot like "looking."

One of the greatest quotes on faith that I have ever read is from the pastor and author A. W. Tozer, who served many years ago in Chicago, Illinois. This quote has sustained me through many hardships. A. W. Tozer said, "Faith is the gaze of the soul upon a saving God."

> **"Faith is the gaze of a soul upon a saving God."**
> **(A.W. Tozer)**

Throughout the Bible, we see "looking" connected with believing and having faith. Faith is the gaze of the soul. Where and how does faith gaze on the Lord? Faith gazes upon the Lord, our saving God, *through prayer*.

One of the greatest times of trial for the nation of Judah took place under the time of their good king, Jehoshaphat.

Judah was attacked by a terrible enemy—the amassed armies of the Moabites and the Ammonites. Their attack was going to be horrific, possibly producing a 100% mortality rate. The people felt powerless. "What can we do against such an enemy?" They were consumed with fear. We understand that, don't we? They felt so powerless against this invading enemy. Then, even though he was afraid, King Jehoshaphat *acted*. He called the people into fasting and prayer. Jehoshaphat himself led them in prayer, and it is one of the most beautiful prayers in the Bible. I want us to focus on one phrase from this prayer. It appears in 2 Chronicles 20:12. Here is what the King of Judah prayed to God:

> "O our God, will you not execute judgment on them? For we are powerless against this great horde that is coming against us. We do not know what to do, but our eyes are on you."

"We do not know what to do but our eyes are on you." Isn't that beautiful? They were looking to God in prayer. Their eyes were on him as they were praying. The people of God kept their eyes closed in prayer, and yet in the spiritual world, their eyes were "opened" to see the Lord. As they closed their eyes in prayer, their eyes were opened in prayer to see the greatness of their God. They were encouraged by seeing him and it gave them faith to act. And as they responded in faith, God gave one of the greatest victories his people had ever known.

So, yet again remember our question—what is faith? Faith is gazing upon God in prayer. That is how we express faith. We gaze upon God in prayer. But faith is also expressed by focusing on God's Word. In John, Chapter 3, Jesus describes faith as the *gaze of the soul*. Nicodemus, one of the rulers of the Jewish people, came to Jesus in the dark of night. He was a good man, a devout man, but with regard to his relationship with God, he had no peace in his heart. Jesus said to him, "Nicodemus, you must be born again." And Nicodemus replied, "How is this possible? How can a man be born again when he is old?" Jesus directed Nicodemus to the Word of God, and this Jewish leader learned a lesson that we need to learn right now—Faith is gazing upon a saving God in his Word.

Faith is gazing upon a saving God in his Word.

That is how we find faith—by gazing into the Word of God. What did Jesus tell Nicodemus? We all know the beloved words of John 3:16, yes, but what comes just before verse 16? They are Jesus' words about the way of the new birth.

> "And as Moses lifted up the serpent in the wilderness, so must the Son of Man be lifted up, that whoever believes in him may have eternal life. For God so loved the world, that he gave his only Son, that whoever believes in him should not perish but have eternal life." (John 3:14-16)

Jesus directed this religious leader, this very learned man, to the Word of God. The Lord is reminding Nicodemus of the events recorded in Numbers, Chapter 21, describing the plague of poisonous serpents invading the camp of the Israelites because of their rebellion against God.

> From Mount Hor they set out by the way to the Red Sea, to go around the land of Edom. And the people became impatient on the way. And the people spoke against God and against Moses, "Why have you brought us up out of Egypt to die in the wilderness? For there is no food and no water, and we loathe this worthless food." Then the Lord sent fiery serpents among the people, and they bit the people, so that many people of Israel died. And the people came to Moses and said, "We have sinned, for we have spoken

against the Lord and against you. Pray to the Lord, that he take away the serpents from us." So Moses prayed for the people. And the Lord said to Moses, "Make a fiery serpent and set it on a pole, and everyone who is bitten, when he sees it, shall live." So Moses made a bronze serpent and set it on a pole. And if a serpent bit anyone, he would look at the bronze serpent and live. (Num. 21:4-9)

The people were being attacked by serpents. Many were dying, some were already dead, and all were terrified. They cried out in desperation to the Lord, and the Lord responded to them by instructing Moses to make a serpent out of bronze and raise it up on a pole in the midst of the camp of Israel. Every Jewish person who looked to that serpent was healed.

Jesus cited this story and in effect said, "Nicodemus, that is how you are born again. You must look. You must believe." Just as the Israelites looked to that serpent, we too must look to the Son of God. Once again, Jesus is connecting *believing* and *looking*.

So, once again, what is faith? It is the gaze of the soul on a saving God. And where do we see him? By faith, we "see" God in prayer, and we "see" God's face in Jesus Christ who can only be found in the Word of God. Looking to Jesus is how we believe. It is how our faith is created.

Looking to Jesus is how faith is created.

In times of trial of our faith, when we are so susceptible to the virus of fear, I challenge us all to look with our eyes on our God by closing our eyes in prayer. Let us confess that there are times when we don't know what to do. But in those times, may our eyes be fixed on Jesus. May we truly *look* with faith into the Word of God. Not just read it, not just have our devotions, but may we ask the Lord to help us to see him in his Word.

WHERE DOES FAITH LOOK?

We have discussed what faith is, and how faith is created, but let us now look at where faith focuses. The answer can be found in the words of Hebrews 12:1-2. Here we find a beautiful and amazing image of "gazing upon Jesus." Faith gazes upon a saving God, and that saving God is our Jesus. Our faith is created and sustained as we focus on him. We are enabled by the grace of God to gaze upon him. As we gaze on Christ, we discover that he is the source of our faith. I encourage you to look at the phrase again, read it aloud, and listen to your own voice affirming the Word of God.

"Looking to Jesus, the founder and perfecter of our faith."

The word "founder" is from the Greek word "arxagon." We get our English word "architect" from this source. As we look to Jesus, he is the founder of our faith. So, where do we find faith? We find faith in the founder of our faith. Like an architect, he designs and builds faith in us as we gaze upon him. In fact, the Lord "tears down" the old life and builds us new through faith as we focus our gaze upon him.

The chorus of the old gospel hymn "Turn Your Eyes Upon Jesus," written by Helen Howarth Lemmel, is so true:

> Turn your eyes upon Jesus
> Look full, in his wonderful face
> And the things of earth will grow strangely dim
> In the light of his glory and grace

Jesus is the source of our faith, yes, but he is also the *sustainer* of our faith. We are to look unto Jesus because he is the founder and the perfecter of our faith (Hebrews 12:2). "Perfecter" means that he is the completer. Isn't this great news? He has begun this work of faith in us and he will complete it until the day of Jesus Christ as Paul tells us in Philippians 1:6.

> And I am sure of this, that he who began a good work in you will bring it to completion at the day of Jesus Christ.

Jesus will cause our faith to hold fast. He will cause our faith to grow as we look to him, and yet, all the while, it is Jesus himself who sustains us.

In the midst of trials, we are enabled to persevere in the faith. Jesus said, "In the world you will have tribulation. But take heart; I have overcome the world" (John 16:33). In Scripture, our journey is so often described as one of hardship and trials. And yet, in the crucible of challenges, our faith holds and is sustained as we focus on the Lord Jesus Christ. He is the founder, perfecter, and the protector of our faith. And it is God's grace that causes us to *continue to look* to Jesus. We must remember that faith is not looking once, and then looking away. We are called to gaze upon him, to focus our eyes upon him, because our faith must have a focus.

Jesus Christ is the focus of our faith.

By focusing on Jesus we are able to persevere in faith because our Lord inspires us. He is the surpassing inspiration of our faith. Why should we follow Jesus in times like this? Why should we *ever* follow Jesus? *Because it is Jesus we get to follow.* He is the pearl of great price. (Matt. 13:45) He is the treasure hidden in the field. (Matt. 13:44) He is the inexpressible gift of gracious God almighty. (2 Cor. 9:15) He is the lily of the valley, the fairest of 10,000 to our souls. There is no one like him. When we look to him, we come to know him, and as we come to know him, we love him.

UNHELPFUL WEIGHTS & UNHOLY SIN

Our text in Hebrews 12:1 teaches us that looking to Jesus is also the source of our sanctification. As we focus on him and follow him, he helps us to put aside weights and sins that hinder our journey. A weight is something that is *unhelpful*. It may not be a sin but it is not helpful. It holds us down and holds us back. As we focus on the Lord Jesus, and we pray and are in the Word, he will reveal to us the things that are weighing us down and are unhelpful. But he also helps us to see the things that are actual "sin." Sin is that which is *unholy*. It is not something that is just unhelpful. A sin is actually unholy; it is contrary to God and his nature. Sin is described in this verse as clinging to us. The author refers to sin as if it is a garment wrapped tightly around us. However, by the grace of God, we have the power to strip it off. God, through the gift of repentance, will help us to lay aside everything that is unhelpful, and by his grace, to strip off that which is unholy.

Sometimes we need brothers and sisters to help us, as they speak into our lives and challenge us to grow in grace. True friends can identify what is unhelpful and unholy. We have the ability, even in days of "social distancing," through the extraordinary resources of social media and networking, to build a community that can encourage each other in our walk with the Lord. We can discuss with fellow trusted Christians, our trials and tribulations regarding our journey with Jesus Christ. We are on a journey of following Christ but we are not to travel in isolation.

Ultimately, it is love that keeps us looking to Jesus. However, it is not *our* love; it is *his* love. It is the love of Christ that holds us fast and sustains us. Not our love for him; his love for us. In this coronavirus season, what keeps us "love controlled" when so many seem to be "fear controlled?" What can possibly keep us "love controlled?" One thing and one thing only—*Corona Victus*. The one who wore the crown for you and me, can and will save us. Even though Jesus despised the shame, when we look to him we understand that it was "the joy that was set before him" that enabled him to endure the cross. Jesus saw an all-surpassing joy. Not the joy of the cross. The cross was terrifying and horrible to him, but he went to the cross anyway for the joy that was *beyond* the cross. It was for the joy of his Father glorified and the joy of the children of God brought back to the Father. His image-bearers would be restored, and the paradise that was lost would be regained. Jesus saw the result of his death on the cross and it filled him with joy. Jesus saw you and me, and he saw what we could be if he would go to the cross, and with joy he did it!

It is love that keeps us controlled in a season of fear. Love. Are you feeling fear right now? Solution—think about the love of the one who wore the crown. Think of Jesus Christ. He *wore the crown* because he *bore our sins*, and when we focus our minds on this, on what he did for us, he fills us with love.

Horatio G. Spafford, the author of these lyrics, captures the essence of this joy so well in the song, "It Is Well With My Soul."

> My sin—oh, the bliss of this glorious thought!—
> My sin, not in part but the whole,
> Is nailed to the cross, and I bear it no more,
> Praise the Lord, praise the Lord, O my soul!

It can be well with your soul today if you look to Jesus Christ. Gaze upon Christ in faith and it will be well with your soul. You will be completely healed. You may feel the poison of sin in your veins, but if you will look to Jesus he will be your Savior. When he gave his life for you, he was lifted up. Look to him and be saved. Look to the Lord Jesus Christ, brothers and sisters, and be convinced once again that he is worth it. He is the founder and the perfecter of our faith. Yes, there are times when we don't know what to do, but we can pray to him and say, "Our eyes are fixed upon you, Lord. Take us through the valley."

As we gaze upon the Lord in prayer and in the Word, he gives us faith, sustains our faith, and captures our hearts in love. The Lord Jesus wore the crown of thorns on the cross and he wears the Victor's crown now in heaven. Take a moment to re-ignite your heart in faith and love by reading aloud the gracious, gospel truth from Hebrews 12:2:

> Looking to Jesus, the founder and perfecter of our faith, who for the joy that was set before him endured the cross, despising the shame, and is seated at the right hand of the throne of God.

PRAYER

Lord, we ask for your grace to sustain us. Thank you for beginning the work in our hearts, bringing us to see the glory of God in the face of Jesus Christ. Oh Lord, help us to fix our eyes on Jesus. And Lord, fill us with your love that, come what may, we will follow our Lord and Savior Jesus Christ. Thank you that wherever he leads us, he leads us in love, mercy, strength, truth, and grace. Thank you, Jesus, that you are leading us...home.

Amen.

R.E.A.P. GUIDE

READ
- Read Hebrews 12:1-2.
- What do you think the Holy Spirit intends to teach us from this passage?

EXAMINE
- "Therefore" (12:1) connects those in the Hall of Faith (Heb. 11) to all followers of Jesus who walk by faith with him today. How are the faithful in Hebrews 11 described in this verse? In what way do they encourage believers today?
- What are the two commands beginning with "let us?"
- What type of race is *living by faith* compared to what is described in verse 1?
- How is sin described in verse 1? How does sin "cling so closely" to believers?
- Believers are commanded to run the race by "looking to Jesus" (12:2). Reflect on all that you have learned about Jesus and the encouragement believers have by looking to him.

APPLY
- The Lord Jesus endured so much for his people! Have you been tempted to focus on your problems, whether they be small or big? What will you focus on about the Lord Jesus to help you have faith through your difficulties?
- In what ways do you see sin "cling so closely" to you and those around you during times of isolation? What help do you need and what help can you commit to being to others?

- In this time of social distancing, we need to see beyond ourselves and our unique challenges. Considering the reality of persecuted believers and the cause of witnessing for Christ, what types of prayer requests should we be praying for ourselves and others?

PRAY
- Using the "PRAY" acronym, respond with **P**raise to the Lord, **R**epent of sins this Bible passage has revealed to you, **A**sk the Lord for any requests you have, and **Y**ield to his will.

- 3 -

Is Good Friday, Good?

Then the soldiers of the governor took Jesus into the governor's headquarters, and they gathered the whole battalion before him. And they stripped him and put a scarlet robe on him, and twisting together a crown of thorns, they put it on his head and put a reed in his right hand. And kneeling before him, they mocked him, saying, "Hail, King of the Jews!" And they spit on him and took the reed and struck him on the head. And when they had mocked him, they stripped him of the robe and put his own clothes on him and led him away to crucify him.
(Matt. 27:27-31)

Is it Good Friday? That is the question I asked of the congregation as I began my message on Good Friday, April 10, 2020. What follows in the pages of this chapter is the message I shared with the online audience that Good Friday evening. My prayer is that some of the things I communicated on that occasion will minister to your heart on whatever day you read these pages.

Is Good Friday, good? Can we really call it Good Friday when 101 days into 2020 there are 1,688,145 people sickened around the world from the coronavirus and 102,209 have died in this pandemic? Is it Good Friday in the United States, when in 42 days since the first confirmed death from the virus 495,788 of our fellow citizens are now sick and 18,430 have died? Is it Good Friday? When in three weeks, 17 million Americans have lost their jobs and 10 percent of our nation's workforce is unemployed, is it really Good Friday?

Hundreds of millions of believers like us around the world cannot gather on this holy day, on this holy weekend, in houses of worship. Thousands of people have been separated from loved ones who are in hospitals and care facilities. Grieving families have been unable to mourn together and bury their dead together. Schools closed, businesses shuttered, playgrounds empty. So many of you have in many different ways, had your lives turned upside down. Is it Good Friday? At noon today, I prayed with a sister in Christ, a member of my own church family, who was grieving the passing of her dear father. This afternoon, in seeking some time of solitude, I walked through a cemetery and passed a child-sized coffin sitting alone, ready to be lowered into the ground. So, let me ask you one more time: Is it Good Friday?

In a world ravaged by the coronavirus, what could possibly make it Good Friday? Only one thing, and that, my friend, is the reality of *Corona Victus*—the reality of the one who wore the crown on *that* first Good Friday and the reality of the one who still wears the crown on *this* Friday. So to answer the question: Yes, *it surely* is Good Friday!

As we consider these verses in Matthew, Chapter 27, let us focus on the *Crowned One*—the one who was victorious over death and sin on that first Good Friday. The one who finished the work that the Father gave him to do. Let our thoughts be drawn to him, and let us think about the *crown* that he wore. If we will take some time to reflect on what Jesus did that day, nearly 2,000 years ago, we can know, in spite of all things, that yes, it is Good Friday.

THE CROWN OF SCORN

The crown that Jesus wore was a crown of thorns, but it was intended as a *crown of scorn*. Into the mind of one of those Roman soldiers, came the idea—to devise the ultimate scorn of shame that they could place on the head of the one who claimed to be the King of the Jews. However, that sinister scheme did not begin in the heart of that Roman soldier. Oh, no. That scheme began in the depths of the fiend of hell himself—Satan—who hated the Lord Jesus Christ with all his might. The soldiers laughed as they scoffed, slapped, and spit upon the King of the Jews, but encircling them as they did this, were the howling hordes of hell. They gleefully poured out eons of hatred and venom into the face of the one who was crowned with thorns.

The Roman soldiers hated the Jews. To show their disgust for being stationed in Jerusalem (a godforsaken place), they laughed in cruel mockery, they bent their knees, they bowed their heads, and they pledged their loyalty to the king of the Jews. But their words and actions were completely unattached to their wills. They would never surrender their will to Jesus so instead, they sarcastically placed a crown of scorn upon his head.

In a much more subtle and "respectable" way, there are millions, still, this day, who place the crown of scorn on the brow of Jesus. These are people who honor Jesus with their lips, but their hearts are far from him. (Matt. 15:8) God forbid that there would be some reading these pages who would be numbered with those Roman soldiers. That sin would be far greater than that of the soldiers who scorned Jesus in their disbelief and their lack of understanding. How much more grievous is the sin of those *who know* Jesus to be Lord, yet stubbornly and consistently refuse to surrender to him.

But God be praised that the one who bore the crown of scorn still has a heart that beats with compassion and mercy, whose prayer then was, "Father, forgive them, for they know not what they do" (Luke 23:34). Thank God for such a King who, though he was so scorned, yet in his amazing grace still freely forgives those who, like the centurion, will say from their heart, "Truly this [is] the Son of God" (Matt. 27:54).

THE CROWN OF SUBSTITUTION

Yes, we can declare that it is Good Friday because Jesus willingly wore the crown of scorn placed on him by the Roman soldiers. But, that crown was also a *crown of substitution*. Jesus did not deserve this crown, yet he wore it in the place of one who was called Barabbas. In Matthew 27:16, the Bible tells us that a notorious, infamous prisoner named Barabbas was on the top of the Sanhedrin's most wanted list. In Judea, Barabbas was public enemy number one. Barabbas was feared and hated by his own people and also by the Romans.

Other gospel accounts tell us that Barabbas was a murderer and a robber. Jesus wore the crown that Barabbas so completely deserved because he was the king of the criminals. Barabbas deserved the crown. But on that first Good Friday, Jesus wore Barabbas's crown. It was Barabbas's scourging that Jesus endured. It was Barabbas's cross that Jesus bore. It was Barabbas's spikes that pierced Jesus' body. It was Barabbas's execution that Jesus endured. Jesus was Barabbas's substitute.

Jesus died in that sinner's place. Was it Good Friday? Not for Jesus. But it was Good Friday for Barabbas.

For a moment let us take a closer look at Barabbas. Doesn't he look somewhat familiar to you? Haven't you seen him before? Take a good look at him and then take a good look at his name. His name is Barabbas or literally Bar-Abbas, which means "son of the father." And did any son ever dishonor his father's name more terribly than Barabbas?

But Barabbas was an image-bearer. He was made in the image of God. He was made in the likeness of the Lord, but Barabbas wasted his entire life living in rebellion against the one whose very image he bore. He hated the one who would give his life for him. Who more justly deserved condemnation and execution? But it did not happen for Barabbas because someone took his place. Who did that? We know who did that —Jesus. My friend, Jesus is the true Barabbas. He is the true "Son of the Father." He is *the* Son of God.

Each one of us could benefit greatly by taking a closer look at Barabbas because in so many ways he is more than familiar. If we have the courage to look, we will find that in reality, Barabbas is identical to *us*. As a matter of fact, each of us is Barabbas. I am Barabbas and you are Barabbas. We are made in the image of the Father, yes. We bear the likeness of the Lord, but each of us has been robbers of our own birthright. We have rebelled against our Heavenly Father and are murderers of his Son, who was crucified for our crimes.

Yet, *it was* Good Friday because it was the injustice of Jesus' execution that satisfied the justice of God upon our sin. It was the injustice of Jesus' execution that God used to execute his justice that was so due upon our sin. It was through amazing grace that, by his stripes and wounds we have been healed. (Isa. 53:5) The "Heavenly Barabbas," the true Son of the Father who died, willingly exchanged his life, the just for the unjust, that he might bring us to God. (1 Pet. 3:18) Jesus, the true Barabbas, took our place so that we might be set free from death row. And we might become the heavenly Barabbas.

Jesus died for us so that we could become true sons and daughters of the Father now and forevermore. Yes, it was Good Friday because Jesus wore the *crown of substitution*.

Events that occurred on that first Good Friday had never been more wrong. The arrest was wrong. The trial was wrong. The interrogation was wrong. The torture was wrong. The judgment was wrong. The execution was wrong. The murder was wrong. It was all wrong. But...it was *all right*. It was all completely right in the sovereign plan of God because *Jesus was completely in control*. His crown of thorns was a crown of sovereignty.

THE CROWN OF SOVEREIGNTY

If we had been there the night that Jesus was so abused or the day that Jesus was nailed to the cross, we would have thought that things were completely out of control. But throughout this shameful ordeal, as Jesus wore those crown of thorns, he also wore the *crown of sovereignty*. Jesus was in complete control. He was in control of all of the events that night and all of the events that morning.

Jesus was not on trial. In reality, mankind was on trial. Jesus was put under oath. The high priest challenged him by an oath that he testify whether he was the Son of God, and Jesus rightly and truly declared that *he was*. He was interrogated by that prideful, coward Pontius Pilot, who asked him, "Are you a king?" Jesus answered, "My kingdom is not of this world. If my kingdom were of this world, my servants would have been fighting, that I might not be delivered over to the Jews. But my kingdom is not from the world" (John 18:36). Jesus is the King but his kingdom is not of this world.

You see, Jesus was in control that day. He was in control of events but he was also in control of *himself*. By his own testimony, he could have asked the Father and thousands of legions of angels would have come to his rescue, but Jesus did not ask for angels to deliver him. He begged for strength to do the will of God.

Jesus *wanted* to do God's will.

Jesus was in control of himself. He did not return accusation for accusation. Even as he was abused, Jesus did not defend himself. He committed himself to the one who judges righteously.

Jesus also did not reject the pitiful cry for mercy from the criminal hanging beside him on the cross. The same criminal who had ridiculed Jesus and cursed him moments before, by God's grace suddenly recognized Jesus as the Messiah. Hanging there beside him, he begged, "Jesus, remember me when you come into your kingdom." And Jesus replied, "Truly, I say to you, today you will be with me in paradise" (Luke 23:42-43). Jesus was in control.

Jesus' life was not taken. No one took the life of Jesus. Jesus laid his life down, willingly, for sinners like you and me. Jesus was in total control. It was Good Friday, and when everything was wrong, when nothing made sense, when it was truly the world's darkest hour, *Jesus was in control*. Nearly 2,000 years later, Jesus is still in control. He wears the crown and it is the crown of *absolute sovereignty*. Life is not always good but Jesus always is.

Life is not always good but Jesus always is.

And *in* him and *through* him, it can always be Good Friday. In Jesus Christ our Lord, who has conquered death for us, who lives on our behalf, and who is coming for us one day, *every day* is Good Friday. May we worship this wonderful crowned Lord even as we study his Word and give him thanks.

Friends, during this coronavirus epidemic we may be separated physically from one another. And certainly, when we pass through life's storms, we sometimes *feel* separated from

God's love. But through dark seasons, we can thank our blessed God that he is in all places, at all times, and we are never, ever alone.

We are never, ever alone.

PRAYER

Sovereign Lord, we thank you that you never leave us or forsake us. We praise your name for what you accomplished through your Son on Good Friday—the momentous event that truly made every day a "Good Day" for us, your redeemed children. On that darkest of all days, you sent out the light of your salvation to the ends of the earth. We praise you, O, Lord, for the moment in each of our lives that you shined your saving grace into the darkness of our hearts and caused us to see the light of the knowledge of your glory in the face of Jesus Christ. Jesus, may the radiance of your face always be before us as we journey through the dark seasons of life. May you brighten our path through the light of your Word. May our minds be forever fixed on you through faith. And may we always and only worship you, our Savior, King and living Lord, Jesus Christ.

Amen.

R.E.A.P. GUIDE

READ
- Read Matthew 27:11-31.
- What do you think the Holy Spirit intends to teach us from this passage?

EXAMINE

On Palm Sunday, we remember the event when Jesus rode into Jerusalem on the back of a colt. People cried "Hosanna," which means "save now, we pray!" On this day, the people honored Jesus as a king. How different is this scene of Jesus' life compared to just a few days later in Matthew 27?

- As Jesus stood trial before Pilate, what question is he asked (11)? His answer, "You have said so," was used to put the burden of answer back on the questioner. Why did Jesus do this?
- Verses 15-26 describe the scene of Jesus and Barabbas. How is Jesus described, and what happens to him in this scene?
- Verses 27-31 tell of the mockery Jesus endured, the public shame, and the abuse. For what in particular were the soldiers mocking Jesus? What is the irony here?
- Read in conclusion Revelation 19:11-16. The image of Jesus has changed dramatically. How is he described here?

APPLY
- What are your personal takeaways from these accounts of the life of Jesus?
- What message can we apply from these texts to circumstances we face in the coronavirus pandemic?

PRAY
- Using the "PRAY" acronym, respond with **P**raise to the Lord, **R**epent of sins this Bible passage has revealed to you, **A**sk the Lord for any requests you have, and **Y**ield to his will.

- 4 -

THE CONQUEROR OF DEATH

I, John, your brother and partner in the tribulation and the kingdom and the patient endurance that are in Jesus, was on the island called Patmos on account of the word of God and the testimony of Jesus. I was in the Spirit on the Lord's day, and I heard behind me a loud voice like a trumpet saying, "Write what you see in a book and send it to the seven churches, to Ephesus and to Smyrna and to Pergamum and to Thyatira and to Sardis and to Philadelphia and to Laodicea." Then I turned to see the voice that was speaking to me, and on turning I saw seven golden lampstands, and in the midst of the lampstands one like a son of man, clothed with a

> long robe and with a golden sash around his chest. The hairs of his head were white, like white wool, like snow. His eyes were like a flame of fire, his feet were like burnished bronze, refined in a furnace, and his voice was like the roar of many waters. In his right hand he held seven stars, from his mouth came a sharp two-edged sword, and his face was like the sun shining in full strength. When I saw him, I fell at his feet as though dead. But he laid his right hand on me, saying, "Fear not, I am the first and the last, and the living one. I died, and behold I am alive forevermore, and I have the keys of Death and Hades.
> (Rev. 1:9-18)

What a strange and different Easter 2020 has ushered in for millions of believers looking for fellowship and celebration on the most important day of the Christian Church. This year our churches are empty. But regardless, it is still a wonderful Easter because even though most of our churches are empty, our hearts are full because *his tomb is empty.* Worship on Easter for the followers of the Lord is always full because Jesus' tomb is empty. No matter the trials, the truth remains the same—Jesus is alive!

Jesus is alive and the coronavirus cannot infect and it cannot weaken our praise to *Corona Victus*—the one who wears the crown. Jesus is the victor because he has overcome sin, death, and Hades, and he is alive forevermore. In a time of coronavirus, we worship on Easter Sunday, *Corona Victus*—the mighty conqueror, Jesus Christ.

And that same living Christ illumines all our darkness, just as he illuminated the cave of the Apostle John who was imprisoned on the Isle of Patmos. He was banished there because of his faithfulness to the gospel and his testimony for Jesus Christ. The Roman emperor Domitian believed that this old man in his mid to late 80's was finished; his ministry would no longer be a threat to the peace of the empire and before long he would be dead, worked to death in the mines of Patmos.

But that was far from the case. Perhaps the greatest ministry of the Apostle John was granted to him when he wrote from banishment on Patmos the words contained in our Bibles as the Book of the Revelation. He was imprisoned, yes. His cell was a tiny cave, but his dark cave was illuminated when he saw his Master, the *Conqueror of Death*. I pray that we as well, by the Spirit's grace, will see Jesus afresh and anew in the light of his revelation in this passage as the one who remains the conqueror of death.

JESUS IS THE LORD OF GLORY

When Jesus manifested himself to John in that cave, how different he appeared. Jesus revealed himself to John as the Lord of Glory. We are told of the incredible impact on John when he sees his beloved Savior in all his majesty. John fell at Jesus' feet as though he were dead. That is his own testimony in Rev. 1:17, "When I saw him, I fell at his feet as though dead." How amazing that is! Think of it; this is the Apostle John. This is the disciple who was closest to Jesus. This is the disciple who laid his head on Jesus' chest at the Last Supper, the night before our Lord was crucified. This is the disciple who is called, of all the disciples—*the disciple whom Jesus loved*. This is the disciple, so close to Jesus, that in Jesus' dying moments he entrusts him with the care of his mother. John knew Jesus. He *really* knew Jesus, yet in his presence, when John sees Jesus in all of his glory, he collapses before him like a dead man.

When John saw the glorified Christ that day, he beheld unveiled Deity. That word *unveiled* is important. It actually is the meaning of the word *revelation*. This last book in our Bibles is titled, The Revelation of Jesus Christ but the words actually mean *the unveiling of Jesus Christ*. In the words of this final epistle written by the last of the apostles, Jesus Christ is unveiled in all of his eternal glory.

When John looks on Jesus, he sees him as having eyes shining with the fire of omniscience. He hears him with a voice that is resounding with the power of omnipotence. He sees him as having hair, not brown as a young man, but gleaming white with the years of eternity. John sees Jesus with feet that are blazing with the purity of justice and judgment.

You see, the veil of time and space had been lifted, and unveiled before John was the Great I Am, the Lord of Glory, the Prince of Life. For John it was just too much; he collapsed like one who had been struck dead.

But this experience reveals something else to John. He not only sees Jesus in his unveiled deity, but John also *sees himself* in his *unworthy humanity*. John collapses before the unveiled deity as a sinner struck down by the awesome holiness of God because he is able to see himself clearly in his unworthy humanity.

Now, remember, John is in his late 80's. He is a good man; there was none better than John. He is a godly man who loves the Lord Jesus with all his heart, soul, mind, and strength. John has been a faithful servant of Jesus' since the days of his youth—for at least 65 years. But before the risen Lord of Glory, John is so overcome by the consciousness of his own insignificance and the awareness of his own sinfulness that he falls at the feet of Jesus like a dead man.

Throughout the Bible, we see this repeated that those who knew the Lord most intimately were awe-struck when they actually saw him in his majesty. Let's reflect on the response of some of the individuals and their own "close encounter of the divine kind." Consider Daniel, for instance. When Daniel saw the Son of Man he said, "I was frightened and fell on my face" (Dan. 8:17). Isaiah had a similar experience when in a glorious vision he beheld the Lord of Glory and cried out, "Woe is me! For I am lost; for I am a man of unclean lips, and I dwell in the midst of a people of unclean lips; for my eyes have seen the King, the Lord of hosts!" (Isa. 6:5)

When Elijah, the great prophet, heard only the *whispering* voice of Jehovah in that cave, he wrapped himself in a cloak and covered his face. Abraham, was known as the friend of the Lord, yet in the Lord's presence he confessed, "Behold, I have undertaken to speak to the Lord, I who am but dust and ashes" (Gen. 18:27). And consider Peter, the leader of the disciples. When he understood the Lord of creation was in his fishing boat, "he fell down at Jesus' knees, saying, 'Depart from me, for I am a sinful man, O Lord'" (Luke 5:8). Yes, the people who knew the Lord best were at times overwhelmed in his presence.

This reminds me of a saying often repeated by wheat farmers in the mid-west, "The head of wheat that is the fullest, bends the lowest."

The head of wheat that is the fullest, bends the lowest.

The mind that is filled with the glory of the Lord Jesus Christ will bend very low in his presence. The person who truly knows Christ knows him for who he is and also knows his own place in comparison. A person who truly knows the Lord Jesus Christ knows that next to Jesus his or her own place is a place of humility and a place of worship and adoration. When in the Lord Jesus Christ's presence, the only place we belong is at his feet. Brothers and sisters, may that be *our* place. If it has not been our place recently, may it be our place today, right now. May we come, once again, humbly before the Lord Jesus Christ.

JESUS IS THE LORD OF GRACE

Sixty years had passed since John had seen Jesus, and now in a matter of moments, he comes face-to-face with the

Lord of Glory and falls at his feet as dead. Then occurs one of the most beautiful, touching things recorded anywhere in Scripture. While this old, gray-haired man was bowed like a dead man before the feet of the Lord of Glory, Revelation 1:17 says, "But he laid his right hand on me, saying, 'Fear not.'" Gray-headed old John is lying prostrate before the Lord, and then he feels a touch. It is a touch that he has not felt in over 60 years, but it is a familiar touch to every fiber of his being. It is the touch of his Master's hand. He remembers that touch and he hears that voice and yes, it is a majestic voice, but in its majesty, it is warm and gentle. It is the voice that he remembers so well, the voice of his beloved friend, Jesus that says to him, "Fear not."

What a wonderful truth for us to claim today—the truth that our Savior Jesus Christ is the Lord of Glory. Yes. He is the risen one. But he is also the Lord of Grace. "Fear not," is what Jesus said. "Fear not" is still the message of the Lord of Glory. Those words told John something he needed to know so desperately—that the *sovereign* Lord Jesus was the same Lord Jesus. *He was still the same.*

Jesus is still the same.

The Jesus we read about in the gospel is *still the same*. He has not changed. He has changed in the outward display of his glory, yes, but his nature has not changed. His identity has not changed. And thank God, his heart has not changed. *He is still the same.* His hands that hold the stars, and they do, are the same hands that touched the leper. His hands are the same hands that blessed the children. And his nail-scarred hands that are omnipotent are the same hands that were nailed to the cross for you and me.

His eyes, do flame with omniscience, but they are the same eyes that wept over Jerusalem, and the same eyes that tenderly looked upon his disciples. His feet that are like fiery brass, are the same feet that staggered and stumbled up the hill of Calvary and to the cross. He is still the same. Lord Jesus is still the same yesterday, today, and forever. Praise God for that! And, his message is still the same. It is still the same to us today as it was to John on the Isle of Patmos–"Fear not." What a great and wonderful word for us on this Easter *of all Easters*, maybe the most unique of all of our experience—Fear not!

We do not need to fear life because Jesus says, "I am the first and the last, and the living one. I died, and behold I am alive forevermore" (Rev. 1:17-18). As Christians, we do not have to be overcome with fear in life because we have a Master who has overcome death and lives forever. He tells us, "Fear not." His everlasting arms protect us. His everlasting presence pacifies our troubled hearts. His everlasting intercession, before his Father, pleads for us even now. We need not fear life.

And *we also do not need to fear death*. Jesus said to John, "Fear not, I have the keys of Death and Hades" (Rev. 1:18). A key is a symbol of authority. Jesus is saying, "I have authority over death." Our Lord has authority over death because he *conquered* death. He is *Corona Victus* because he conquered death by his resurrection, and he took away the key from the prince of death—Satan. For Jesus' followers, the door of death holds no fear because the master holds the key to that door of death, and he says, "Fear not." We do not have to fear life and we do not have to fear death. And, because of the Lord Jesus, *we do not have to fear eternity*.

We need not fear life, death, or eternity.

Jesus said, "I have the keys of Death and Hades." In the Bible, Hades is the dwelling place of the spirits of those who have died. And Jesus, by his resurrection, opened the door of eternity to grant eternal life to all who would trust in him. Since Jesus holds in his hand the keys of Hades, we can claim the promise of the Apostle Paul who said that to be absent from this body is to be present with the Lord (2 Cor. 5:8). Death has been defeated and the grave has been conquered.

> Behold! I tell you a mystery. We shall not all sleep, but we shall all be changed, in a moment, in the twinkling of an eye, at the last trumpet. For the trumpet will sound, and the dead will be raised imperishable, and we shall be changed. For this perishable body must put on the imperishable, and this mortal body must put on immortality. When the perishable puts on the imperishable, and the mortal puts on immortality, then shall come to pass the saying that is written: "Death is swallowed up in victory." (1 Cor. 15:51-54)

When we die or when Jesus comes for us, "We will always be with the Lord" (1 Thess. 4:17). What a wonderful promise! That promise once again became so real for my family just a few days ago. This past Monday I stood by my wife Susan as she held the hand of her younger sister, Carol. Carol was just 59 years of age but losing her battle with a terrible illness. I watched as she took her last breath here on earth. Susan held her. Carol took her *last breath on earth*, but her *next breath was in heaven* and in the presence of the Lord. Her faith and trust were in Jesus Christ. She *knew* him. And at that moment she was delivered from her diseased-ridden body and was immediately delivered into the presence of the Lord. She is there today, thank God. We know that with unshakeable confidence because Jesus holds the keys and he says to us, "Fear not."

Those keys are keys *of our deliverance* from the power of Death and Hades. That should fill the heart of every single believer today with such great hope and confidence.

However, if you have not been born again, if you have not turned from your sins and trusted in Jesus Christ and experienced the new birth, those keys in the hands of Jesus are not the keys of your deliverance. They are the keys to your doom. The key in Jesus' hand that unlocks the door to eternal life is the same key that locks the door to eternal doom for those who reject him.

Years ago, a warden holding a key in his hand walked into a prison cellblock. He stopped and stood before a barred and locked cell door and stared at an inmate sitting on his bunk. To the criminal, the warden looked like an angel because it was the day of his release. With that key, the warden opened his cell door and led the convict to freedom. About an hour later the same warden came into the same cellblock, carrying the same key, and he stood before the cell door of another convicted criminal. To that criminal, the warden looked like the angel of death, because with that key the warden had come to open the door and lead the condemned man to his execution. The same warden. The same cellblock. The same key. To one, an opened door of freedom. To the other, an opened door to execution.

This same Jesus which we read about in Scriptures and who is *the liberator* to all who accept him, is also *the executioner* to all who reject him. The door of eternity will close behind them forever and will keep them from the presence of the Lord and the glory of his joy forever. They will reside in a place of eternal doom and punishment for the rest of eternity.

My friend, which will Jesus be for you? Will he be your liberator or will he be your executioner? You might be asking, "Can you know?" I have been asked this countless times over the many years of my ministry, "Sam, can you really know?" And I can tell you with full assurance, "Absolutely, yes!" You can know that Jesus is your liberator and that he has opened the door to freedom for you now and forever. However, you do not have to take the promise of a preacher. You can take the promise of a prisoner to a jailer. What am I talking about? I am sharing with you what the prisoner, the Apostle Paul, promised the jailer at midnight in Philippi when the jailer fell on his knees pleading, "What must I do to be saved?" And Paul, the prisoner who was free in Christ, said to the jailer, who was in the prison of his sin, "Believe in the Lord Jesus, and you will be saved" (Acts 16:31).

"Believe in the Lord Jesus, and you will be saved."

This is the promise of our living Lord, our loving Savior, Jesus Christ. If you will turn from your sin today and trust only in the merit of Jesus Christ who took your place, who died for you, and who rose again for you. If you will put your trust completely in him today, he will set you free. And you will personally experience the blessed reality that when the Son of God sets you free, you are a free man or woman forever and ever. May this be the day of your freedom. Today, Jesus holds the keys and the door of eternal life is open. The Bible ends with the "open-door invitation" of life in the Lord Jesus.

> The Spirit and the Bride say, "Come." And let the one who hears say, "Come." And let the one who is thirsty come; let the one who desires take the water of life without price. (Rev. 22:17)

The door is open and Jesus holds the key. He wears the Victor's crown and he is victorious over Death and Hades. He is *Corona Victus*, and his victory is *your* victory if you trust in him today. Our hope is in Christ alone.

PRAYER

Blessed Master, because of you each day is for us Easter Sunday and the Lord's Day. Your empty tomb is our treasury overflowing with assurances that every promise you have shared with us is true and secure. Because you live, Lord Jesus, we live now in you and will one day live with you forever. Sovereign Lord, you are still the immutable, eternal, omniscient and omnipotent Lord of Glory before whom your disciple, John, fell as though dead. Your holiness is all-consuming, but we trust in your grace that is all-sufficient. Grant to us as we humbly kneel before you in reverent worship, that along with John we may sense in our spirit the same loving touch upon us and hear you, our Prince of Peace, sharing those same blessed words of unspeakable comfort, "Fear not."

Amen.

R.E.A.P. GUIDE

READ
- Read Revelation 1:9-18.
- What do you think the Holy Spirit intends to teach us from this passage?

EXAMINE
- John the apostle was a prisoner on the Isle of Patmos. How does John identify with the churches in his introduction (1:9)?
- While worshiping God on the "Lord's Day" (Resurrection day—Sunday), John hears Jesus calling on him to write down what he hears and to send it to the seven churches. How is Jesus described?
- What message does Jesus have for John in verse 17? Why did John need this message? Jesus also said, "I am the first and the last..." What is the significance of this (compare to Isa. 44:6)?
- What are the four things Jesus reveals about himself in verse 18?
- Anyone who holds the "keys" (Rev. 1:18) has the authority over that person or thing. The key holder determines who gets in and who gets out. Since Jesus has authority over Death and Hades, how does that apply to believers in Jesus now (see Rev. 1:5)?

APPLY
- How do you view the Lord Jesus? When does he seem most distant to you? When does he seem nearest? How does this passage reassure us about Jesus' connection to his people?
- What fears do you deal with in your everyday life? Death and Hell are the biggest threats we will ever face. How

has Jesus dealt with our biggest threats? How should that influence our thinking and outlook today?

PRAY
- Using the "PRAY" acronym, respond with **P**raise to the Lord, **R**epent of sins this Bible passage has revealed to you, **A**sk the Lord for any requests you have, and **Y**ield to his will.

- 5 -

THE VACCINE FOR FEAR

*N*ow when David and his men came to Ziklag on the third day, the Amalekites had made a raid against the Negeb and against Ziklag. They had overcome Ziklag and burned it with fire and taken captive the women and all who were in it, both small and great. They killed no one, but carried them off and went their way. And when David and his men came to the city, they found it burned with fire, and their wives and sons and daughters taken captive. Then David and the people who were with him raised their voices and wept until they had no more strength to weep. David's two wives also had been taken captive, Ahinoam of Jezreel and Abigail the widow of Nabal of Carmel. And David was greatly distressed, for the people spoke of

> stoning him, because all the people were bitter in soul, each for his sons and daughters. But David strengthened himself in the Lord his God. And David said to Abiathar the priest, the son of Ahimelech, "Bring me the ephod." So Abiathar brought the ephod to David. And David inquired of the Lord, "Shall I pursue after this band? Shall I overtake them?" He answered him, "Pursue, for you shall surely overtake and shall surely rescue."
> (1 Sam. 30:1-8)

Around the country, many scientists are fervently working at this time on a vaccine for the dreadful COVID-19 virus. Much prayer is needed for these specialists who are serving our fellow man so diligently. I understand that many of the studies involved in seeking this vaccine have to do with two case study groups. One of the groups includes people who have been exposed to the virus but have not contracted the illness. They are being carefully evaluated as to why they have not come down with the terrible symptoms.

The second group consists of those who have been infected and have developed symptoms but have made a very quick and strong recovery. They are being evaluated as well, in order to understand more about the virus so a vaccine can be developed. All of these studies are ultimately *individual case studies* that can hopefully provide protection for *everyone* from this deadly virus.

Through the Word of God today, let's engage in our own *individual case study* to help us experience the breakthrough of *Corona Victus: Overcoming the Virus of Fear*. Let's take a look into the life of one of God's servants and see how, by God's grace, he was able to gain victory over the terrible virus of fear in his life.

David is the focus of this case study—a faithful servant of God infected with the virus of fear, but one who also experienced a wonderful and amazing deliverance by God. Our case study comes to us during a time in the life of this man who is devoted to God with all his heart. However, David has been infected with the virus of fear and his life is terribly devastated. In 1 Samuel, Chapter 27, we see how this virus first infected the life of such a servant of the Lord.

Now, every one of us is susceptible to fear; not one of us is immune from it. But there is the *right kind* of fear and there is the *wrong kind* of fear. Sometimes people are more vulnerable to the virus of fear when they are experiencing a time of significant fatigue. Physical and emotional fatigue makes us very susceptible to fear, and that is certainly the case with David. David is exhausted physically from relentlessly having to flee from place to place in his efforts to hide from King Saul who seeks his life. David is tired physically and is emotionally drained, and being so physically and emotionally depleted, David becomes a prime candidate for fear.

"Fatigue makes cowards of us all."

I recently read a quote by the great U.S. Army general from World War II, George Patton, who once said, "Fatigue makes cowards of us all." The virus of fear, though, does not begin in a person's feet. It doesn't first display symptoms through running away. That is not the first sign of the virus. No, the virus of fear first manifests itself in a person's brain. Notice the progression of the symptoms of fear in the life of David. We see the first symptoms in the way he is *thinking*. The virus of fear is causing him to think *in the dark*. We are given insight into this in 1 Samuel 27:1

> Then David said in his heart, "Now I shall perish one day by the hand of Saul. There is nothing better for me than that I should escape to the land of the

Philistines. Then Saul will despair of seeking me any longer within the borders of Israel, and I shall escape out of his hand."

Notice that we are told, "David said in his heart." David is talking to *himself*. Someone has wittily said that when you talk to yourself you are probably having a foolish conversation. Well, David is talking to *himself* and he is also *discouraging* himself. He is "thinking" himself into discouragement as he attempts to come up with his own plan to address a very traumatic situation. He very carefully tries to figure out an action plan that makes the most sense to him. Proactively, he takes matters into his own hands. The problem is that he is *planning under the influence*, the influence of fear. In his fear, he is not thinking right and so he comes up with a very *wrong* idea. The root of the problem is that in his fear-driven thinking, he is *robbed of faith*. The virus of fear causes David to forget the promises of God. This is what fear so often does in the life of the believer.

Fear causes us to forget the promises of God.

In his fear, David forgets all the amazing promises God has made to him. First of all, he forgets that he has been chosen by the Lord. God sought David and found David. He is God's anointed one to be the next king of Israel. Person after person has promised David that he is going to be king someday. Samuel, the great prophet, has told David he is going to be king. His best friend, Jonathan, the son of Saul, has told him, "You're going to be the king someday." His wife Abigail has encouraged him, "I know you are going to be the king someday. Even Saul, the one from whom David is fleeing has said to him, "David, you are going to be king someday." But the virus of fear has weakened David's faith by undermining and discounting God's promises.

WEAKENED HIS STANDARDS

Not only did fear weaken David's faith, but the weakening of his faith led to the weakening of his standards. His wrong thinking began to infect the standards of his life which then led to personal compromise. David's thinking in the dark led him to *walking in the dark*.

WALKING IN THE DARK

> So David arose and went over, he and the six hundred men who were with him, to Achish the son of Maoch, king of Gath. And David lived with Achish at Gath, he and his men, every man with his household, and David with his two wives, Ahinoam of Jezreel, and Abigail of Carmel, Nabal's widow. (1 Sam. 27:2-3)

Talk about a detour! All the road signs on David's journey read, "Welcome to Gath!" Remember Gath? Gath is one of the chief cities of the Philistines. It is also the hometown of a man by the name of Goliath. Yes, *that* Goliath—the giant-sized, enemy of God that David, by the grace of God, overcame in battle. Now here is David in his fear, thinking so wrongly, and being so impacted by his fear that he walks into the land of the Philistines, the enemies of God, and *lives with them*!

COMPROMISED HIS CONVICTIONS

The virus of fear has compromised David's entire system of his life. The fear causes him to be compromised in four key areas of his spiritual health. To begin, it causes David to compromise his *convictions*. He is still God's man inwardly—in his heart, and he still loves God. But *outwardly* David has conformed his life to those of the enemies of God. He reasons with himself that it is easier to live like the enemies of God. It is safer to be like them. David has compromised his convictions because of the virus of fear, but he has also *compromised his influence*.

COMPROMISED HIS INFLUENCE

His compromise does not just impact himself; it never does. His compromise involves other people, starting with his family. David had taken his family and his friends into the land of the enemies of God. So, his personal compromise now also involves his friends and their families. David, their leader, has led them all into the land of the enemies of God. What a terrible thing is this virus of fear! It caused David to compromise his convictions, compromise his influence, and notice what it did to his soul. Fear *compromised his fellowship*.

COMPROMISED HIS FELLOWSHIP

> And the number of the days that David lived in the country of the Philistines was a year and four months. (1 Sam. 27:7)

16 months of Philistine living. What do we know about these 16 months? If you study David's life, you will find that he never wrote a single Psalm during this 16-month period. How could he? How could he write the songs of Zion in such a place as Gath? How could he sing or write Psalms of the Lord while living among the enemies of God, compromising his life and the lives of others? How could he experience joy in his heart? Impossible. For 16 months, the greatest songwriter in history wrote no songs.

He compromised his convictions. He compromised his influence. He compromised his fellowship, and most of all (and maybe worst of all), he *compromised his testimony*.

COMPROMISED HIS TESTIMONY

> Now the Philistines had gathered all their forces at Aphek. And the Israelites were encamped by the spring that is in Jezreel. As the lords of the Philistines were passing on by hundreds and by thousands, and David and his men were passing on in the rear with Achish, the commanders of the Philistines said, "What are these Hebrews doing here?" And Achish said to the commanders of the Philistines, "Is this not David, the servant of Saul, king of Israel, who has been with me now for days and years, and since he deserted to me I have found no fault in him to this day." But the commanders of the Philistines were angry with him. And the commanders of the Philistines said to him, "Send the man back, that he may return to the place to which you have assigned him. He shall not go down with us to battle, lest in the battle he become an adversary to us. For how could this fellow reconcile himself to his lord? Would it not be with the heads of the men here? Is not this David, of whom they sing to one another in dances, 'Saul has struck down his thousands, and David his ten thousands'?"
> (1 Sam. 29:1-5)

It is difficult to imagine the complete impact of fear on David's life. He is not just living among the Philistines. We are told in this passage that David has become a *captain* of the Philistines —a leader among them. But notice, although David has *earned a rank* among these people he has not *earned their respect*. What did the Philistines say about David when it came time for battle? They said, "Of all people, what is *he* doing here?" Even the Philistines knew that David should not be there. And you can imagine what *his* men and family are saying? They are probably echoing, "Yes, what *are* we doing here? We don't belong here." David gained a rank but he was neither respected by his enemies nor his friends. That is the detour and the destination of compromise. When we compromise our convictions, we are not respected by our enemies and we are not respected by our friends.

Eventually, the Philistines turned David back. They really didn't trust him and said, "You can't go." But this Philistine's decision was part of God's plan. God is sovereign; he is able to use even his worst enemies to carry out the plans he has made on behalf of his people. These enemies of God, the Philistines, carried out God's plan by turning David back. They were instrumental in bringing David face-to-face with the virus of his compromise, which is exactly what God wanted and what David needed.

SITTING IN THE DARK

David's virus of fear began with "thinking" in the dark. It led him to "walking" in the dark. But now notice the most terrible moment of his life when David finds himself "sitting" in the dark.

> Now when David and his men came to Ziklag on the third day, the Amalekites had made a raid against the Negeb and against Ziklag. They had overcome Ziklag and burned it with fire and taken captive the women and all who were in it, both small and great. They killed no one, but carried them off and went their way. And when David and his men came to the city, they found it burned with fire, and their wives and sons and daughters taken captive. Then David and the people who were with him raised their voices and wept until they had no more strength to weep.
> (1 Sam. 30:1-4)

In these verses, we see David arrive at the awful, final destination on his detour of compromise. This is where the virus of fear has led him. He returns to Ziklag, the town where he has been living with his men, and along with everyone else, looking forward to rejoining their families. However, while he has been gone, the Amalekites have raided and destroyed the city. David has lost everything—his home, his possessions, his family, and his friends. He has reached his lowest point and sits down in the smoking ruin and rubble of his life. The virus of fear which infected David's mind and thinking has now completely devastated his life.

But, thank God, the virus of fear has not hindered the Great Physician in his treatment plan for David's recovery. The Bible tells us that the gifts and the calling of God are irrevocable (Rom. 11:29) and that God will accomplish his purposes in all those he has called to himself (Rom. 8:28). God called David and although David devastated his life with the infection of the virus of fear, the Great Physician had a treatment plan for his recovery. In fact, it was God who *ordained* the consequences of David's poor choices. He did not *cause* David to sin. God is not the author of sin. But God ordained the consequences of David's poor choices so that he would ultimately accomplish his good purposes.

A ministry friend of mine recently recommended that I listen to a message by the noted pastor, Dr. Tony Evans, Senior Pastor of Oak Cliff Bible Church in Dallas, Texas. The message, dated March 22, 2020, is entitled, "Divine Disruptions," and in it, Dr. Evans made a statement that gripped my heart, *"God will let things get as chaotic as they need to be until he gets our undivided attention."* That is so true. God will do whatever necessary to get our attention so that he can correct our vision.

God gets our attention so he can correct our vision.

God often gets our attention through the painful results of the chaos that we bring into our lives so that he can then correct our vision. In the first chapter of this book I made a statement that is important for us to remember, *"God, in his providence, allows us to experience trials so that we learn to view the invisible and to value the invaluable."*

God wants us to have a clear vision. He wants his people to be clear-sighted and see what is real and what truly matters. God wants us to view what is invisible but real so that we can value what is invaluable. And God, at times, allows trials to come into our lives so that he can get our attention and thus correct our vision. He did this for David.

David has reached his *lowest* point but he has also reached his *turning point*. Like the prodigal son of the Old Testament, even though David has devastated his life, (sitting there among the ruin and smoldering ashes of Ziklag) by God's grace David comes to himself. He regains his senses. Things become clear to him. He *remembers*. He has forgotten for 16 long months, but now he remembers who he is. And he remembers *whose he is*. He also remembers *what he has* that cannot be taken away from him. And in that dark moment, David (by God's grace) experiences an amazing recovery.

What radical new treatment was used to recover David from the virus of fear? It is actually an ancient remedy that has timeless effectiveness. The remedy that worked for David 3000 years ago is the timeless medicine of the Lord that is effective to this day for all of us who are in the dark places of fear. By God's grace, David experienced the delivering *vaccine of faith*, and his deadly virus of fear was healed.

THE DELIVERING VACCINE OF FAITH

Notice how wonderfully this vaccine was applied. Although the healing properties are from the Lord by his grace, David self-administers that grace. The answer is from God, the healing is from God, but David *self-administers* the vaccine that God has provided. Notice, David *encouraged himself* in worship.

David encouraged himself through the worship of God.

1 Samuel 30:6 is one of the most remarkable verses in the Bible. David sits in the ruin of Ziklag. Without a doubt, he has lost everything. He has lost his family, and now his friends are talking about stoning him. To quote the title of a book my children often asked me to read to them when they were small —it had been a *terrible, horrible, very bad day*. But notice in 1 Samuel 30:6 what David did on that awful day:

> And David was greatly distressed, for the people spoke of stoning him, because all the people were bitter in soul, each for his sons and daughters. But David strengthened himself in the Lord his God. (1 Sam. 30:6)

Don't miss that. *"But David strengthened himself in the Lord his God."* David changed his focus. His focus was no longer a self-focus. His focus was no longer on the circumstances in his life. This broken man lifted up his eyes to God and the change of focus changed everything. David stopped focusing on what he had lost and started focusing on what *he could not lose*.

David focused on what he could not lose.

The Amalekites had stolen his home, yes. They had stolen his possessions, yes. They have stolen his fortune, yes. They had stolen his family, yes. *But they could not steal his God*. They could take everything else, but they could not take away the relationship he had with his God.

This does not mean that David went into denial. This is not denial. David entered into *reality*—the ultimate reality of God.

The ultimate reality is God.

Regardless of the world's sneering condescension, when in the midst of terrible trial and tribulation, yes, even in the midst of a pandemic, when you go to God you are not going into denial. You are going into reality, my friend. And that is how David returned from his long, dark detour. He came back to reality. He came back to his God and his unchanging love and power. He *remembered* that God was still with him.

During WWII, when so many of London's neighborhoods had been devastated by the Nazi's bombings, people's minds and spirits had been deeply impacted. They had nearly lost all hope. On one occasion, someone took a piece of chalk and wrote over the rubble, "*God is nowhere.*" However, a believer in the Lord upon seeing what had been written, decided to make a *slight* change to the message. Taking another piece of chalk, he marked through "*God is nowhere*" and using the same letters, he wrote, "*God is now here.*" Same situation, but a very different interpretation and realization. Regardless of the nature of the pandemonium or pandemic in which we find ourselves, this is the reality—*God is now here!*

> "Be strong and courageous. Do not fear or be in dread of them, for it is the Lord your God who goes with you. **He will not leave you or forsake you.**"
> (Deut. 31:6)

This is worth repeating over and over again—God will never leave us nor forsake us. Period. God has not abandoned his people. He has not left us. He is here. *God is now here.* David encouraged himself through the worship of his sovereign God. Then David did something more. *He encouraged himself in the worship of God and then he enlightened himself with the Word of God.*

David enlightened himself with the Word of God.

> And David said to Abiathar the priest, the son of Ahimelech, "Bring me the ephod." So Abiathar brought the ephod to David. And David inquired of the Lord, "Shall I pursue after this band? Shall I overtake them?" He answered him, "Pursue, for you shall surely overtake and shall surely rescue."
> (1 Sam. 30:7-8)

The "ephod" was an elaborate mantlepiece or breastplate worn by the high priest. And on the two shoulders of the garment were two precious stones referred to as "Urim and Thummim." These words are believed by many Bible scholars to be best translated, *"Lights and Perfections."* The Bible tells us they were used, at times, to make an inquiry of the Lord—to discern God's will. We are not entirely clear on how that occurred, but it is clear David asked for the ephod because he wanted to inquire of God. He wanted to know God's direction.

This is the first time in 16 months David has done this. Had he gone to God 16 months earlier, prior to deciding on taking *his own path* into Gath, he would have inquired unto the Lord and been guided in God's will. But he didn't. Regardless, God remained faithful, and when David humbly inquired of the Lord, saying, "Should I do this?" God gave him an answer.

In that day, believers used the ephod of God to inquire of the Lord. Today, we do not have the ephod or need the ephod because we have something infinitely better—the Word of God. Yes, we possess the eternal Word of God that is forever settled in heaven to guide us in the way of righteousness. We go to the Word of God because the Bible reveals the mind of the Lord. In his Word, we not only find encouragement but enlightenment in times when we are afraid.

The Bible is the revealed mind of the Lord.

> The law of the Lord is perfect,
>   reviving the soul;
> the testimony of the Lord is sure,
>   making wise the simple;
>
> the precepts of the Lord are right,
>   rejoicing the heart;
> the commandment of the Lord is pure,
>   enlightening the eyes;
> (Ps. 19:7-8)

There have been times when I have actually felt too discouraged to pray. Have you ever felt that way? Perhaps you have felt too discouraged to read the Bible. One can make an excuse saying, "I'm too discouraged to pray. My heart wouldn't be in it. I'm too discouraged to read my Bible. God knows my heart just wouldn't be in it." But that is exactly the point and the opportunity of the Word of God! In times of discouragement, we need to do what pastor and author, Dr. David Jeremiah, calls "spiritual force-feeding." When we don't *feel* like reading the Bible, that is when we need to read it the most! When we don't feel like praying, we absolutely need to pray because that is where and when the Lord will meet us. He will meet us where and when we return to him. We will overcome the deadly spirit of the virus of fear by returning to the Spirit of the Living God.

DOING THE WORD OF GOD

Overcoming the virus of fear requires more than just reading or studying the Word of God. It also requires *doing* the Word of God. David encouraged himself in the *worship of God*, he enlightened himself through the *Word of God*, and then David engaged himself in the *work of God*.

> So David set out, and the six hundred men who were with him, and they came to the brook Besor, where those who were left behind stayed. But David pursued, he and four hundred men. Two hundred stayed behind, who were too exhausted to cross the brook Besor. (1 Sam. 30:9-10)

Notice David's progression in overcoming the virus of fear, he worshiped, he sought the Word of God, he received God's instructions, and then David *obeyed those instructions.*

My friend, you cannot read yourself out of the virus of fear. You cannot pray yourself out of the virus of fear. Yes, we certainly must read the Word of God and we definitely must pray to the Lord our God, but we must also combine, along with prayer and the Word, a personal commitment to *do the work of the Lord.* We must obey what the Lord works into our hearts by doing that which he instructs us to do.

Years ago, a woman asked if she might counsel with me regarding emotional challenges she was experiencing. She was suffering under a spirit of discouragement and fear, continuously overwhelmed by life. She never missed a service at our church. She read her Bible, was involved in several Bible studies and prayed regularly. She also told me that she journaled every day. So after meeting with her a few times, I asked her if she could bring one of her journals into our next meeting. She actually brought several notebooks with page after page completely filled. I took my time and carefully read several pages of her spiritual diary and I found *myself* becoming discouraged! Sadly, this dear lady had turned her worship time and her time of prayer, into a self-absorbed, self-focus. The writings in her journal were all about *her* problems and *her* needs.

The next time we met I told her that I had a homework assignment for her. She was interested so I continued, "Before we meet again, I want you to go down to the Knoxville Area Rescue Mission and serve at least four hours a week." She asked, "Why?" I responded, "It is because you are so absorbed with your *perceived* problems that you need to go *see* and *serve* some dear people who have some *real* problems. As I recall, that was our last session.

May I ask, how are you going to deal with your fear and your discouragement? A bottle of pills? A bottle of Scotch? A six-pack or six scoops? Endlessly flipping through the TV remote? Emptying a bag of chips? Or maybe by a relentless recording and recitation of all your problems to God? Perhaps 17 more Bible studies on spiritual warfare? Or maybe create on Facebook a mutually affirming, network of negativity?

May I save you some time? It will not work. God's spiritual health plan has a key component and that key component is, yes, read the Bible, and yes, pray and worship God, and definitely, attend church regularly. All of these things are awesome but all of these things that are so critically important, will not *in themselves* overcome the virus of fear unless you work a plan which is *a plan to work*. We must implement what we are learning from God if we are going to overcome the virus of fear, grow stronger, and stay healthy. It is not the *hearer* of the Word of God who is blessed, but the *doer* of the Word of God who is blessed. (James 1:25)

**The doer of the Word of God
is richly blessed.**

David gave himself to the work of God. He obeyed, his spirit was revived, and he was set free. David moved from enduring the virus of fear to experiencing the victory of faith.

A VICTORY OF FAITH

Currently, across the nation we hear the cry, "We've got to get the nation back to work!" That certainly is important. We pray for our leaders as they try to determine how the economy should be reopened. Yes, the nation needs to get back to work but may I remind you and me of our *real citizenship*? Our citizenship is in heaven. We *are* citizens of the Kingdom of God. We serve the King and we are never out of work. There is always plenty to do as the people of God. There are countless opportunities. And, the reward is not just in heaven. As we make the focus of our lives doing good, we reward ourselves. We are invited by God to be "Christian hedonists," as pastor and author Dr. John Piper aptly phrases God's command to live for joy. Or, as a dear missionary friend of mine who is now in heaven used to say, we "get in on what God is up to." We overcome the virus of fear as we pour ourselves into the lives of others and in doing so, we bless ourselves.

Recently, I drove into our church's parking lot and an older couple pulled up in a vehicle next to me. Rolling down their window they said, "Pastor Sam, we don't want to bother you, but we forgot it was Saturday and that the church is closed. We have been out grocery shopping and have purchased a few things for Project Jerusalem, the ministry that the church has started for feeding the hungry in our neighborhood. We were wondering if there is any way you could let us into the church." I laughed saying, "Well, I think I may still have a key."

I got out and opened up the door to our children's center and gymnasium while the couple opened up the back of their car. I was amazed. It wasn't just a "few things." The entire back of their car was filled with groceries! I helped them carry them into the building and it was their turn to be amazed when they saw our gym completely filled with food to deliver to our neighbors. When they finished unloading their many bags of grocery items, that couple pulled out of the parking lot rejoicing. They had purchased and provided an expensive load of groceries, but they were all the richer rejoicing in the Lord!

It is believers who are engaged in the *work* of the Lord that experience the *joy* of the Lord. Right now, whether in the midst of a season of pandemic or prosperity, let me encourage you to pause for a moment for self-examination.

A PERSONAL SPIRITUAL HEALTH EVALUATION

Are you exhibiting symptoms of the virus of fear? Have you been thinking and walking and sitting in the dark? Well, my friend, to escape the pandemic of fear you must follow the *vaccination guidelines of faith.*

First of all, *engage yourself in worship.* God is still the same. He is still God. He is still here. He still loves you. The things that are going to last for eternity have not changed. Engage yourself in the changeless love and mercy of God. Secondly, *enlighten yourself in the wisdom of the Word of God.* Be guided, not by circumstances, but by the timeless words of Scripture.

And thirdly, *engage yourself in the work of God.* Look outside yourself and look into your neighborhood or community and think of some ways you can be a blessing to those around you. Write some encouraging notes. Call and check on those you think might be sick physically or struggling emotionally. Pray for people on the phone or by text or email. Go grocery shopping and bring bags of goods to people who might be in need. Contribute financially to those out of work or in need of financial help. Be a witness of your faith and you will find that the God of victory will give you the victory of faith in the midst of your virus of fear.

It is a wonderful and priceless gift to take time out of our isolated, but still busy lives, to admit our need to Jesus. Let's take time to do that right now.

PRAYER

Jesus, we need you every hour. Yes, every hour we need you. We humbly confess this even as we come to you in this hour. We need you, Lord Jesus Christ. You alone are worthy to wear Corona Victus—the Victor's crown. It is only through you that we are able to conquer the virus of fear so filling this world today and often infecting our hearts. Lord, we thank you that we do not have to work "for" victory but "from" victory because of the victory that you accomplished on the cross for us and confirmed in your triumph over the tomb. Lord of the Ages, we praise you that we may call upon you and draw near to you in faith anytime, anywhere. God, you are here. We bless you in Jesus' name.

Amen.

R.E.A.P. GUIDE

READ
- 1 Samuel 30:1-8
- What lessons do you see the Holy Spirit teaching you in this text?

EXAMINE
- Consider the two contrasting examples of King Saul and David. What have you learned about their individual situations and each man's response to that situation?
- What does it mean to "strengthen [oneself] in the Lord his God"? Compare to 1 Samuel 23:16-17. What is the similar phrase there? How did Jonathan encourage David?
- What step did David take to strengthen himself in God (1 Sam. 30:6-8)?

APPLY
- How are you currently experiencing difficulties?
- Who around you is experiencing the heat of stress and difficulty right now?
- Based on the example of David and following his lead, how can you strengthen yourself in the Lord?
- Like Jonathan, how can you strengthen others in the Lord?

PRAY
- Using the "PRAY" acronym, respond with **P**raise to the Lord, **R**epent of sins this Bible passage has revealed to you, **A**sk the Lord for any requests you have, and **Y**ield to his will.

- 6 -

THE THERAPY FOR PEACE

Rejoice in the Lord always; again I will say, rejoice. Let your reasonableness be known to everyone. The Lord is at hand; do not be anxious about anything, but in everything by prayer and supplication with thanksgiving let your requests be made known to God. And the peace of God, which surpasses all understanding, will guard your hearts and your minds in Christ Jesus. Finally, brothers, whatever is true, whatever is honorable, whatever is just, whatever is pure, whatever is lovely, whatever is commendable, if there is any excellence, if there is anything worthy of praise, think about these things. What you have learned and received and heard and

*seen in me—practice these things, and the God of
peace will be with you.*
(Phil. 4:4-9)

Many years ago, my family and I traveled back to Findlay, Ohio, where I once served on a church staff to enjoy some time with our friends there. During our stay, I was invited to participate in a church basketball game between the varsity team of the Christian school and a team consisting of members of the faculty and staff. I was excited to be part of this highly anticipated event.

It was quite a game—back-and-forth. I especially remember a big moment in the game when I was able to steal a pass and dribble up the court for an easy layup. Well, it would have been easy, except that the person from whom I had stolen the ball felt highly motivated to block my shot. However, as I jumped to make the basket, rather than blocking my shot, the other player under-cut my legs and literally sent me into a somersault in the air. I landed on the court on my left arm and immediately knew that something was very wrong. The pain was terrible. Later that evening in the emergency room, the doctor informed me that I had fractured my elbow. Since a cast was not an option, he immobilized my arm in a sling and encouraged me to see my physician when I returned home. A few days later in Knoxville, my primary care doctor arranged for me to have physical therapy at the Baptist Hospital. When I arrived at the older facility, I found to my dismay that the physical therapy department was located in the basement of the hospital, but not just the basement, the *sub-basement,* aka "*dungeon.*" As I recall, there were all kinds of instruments of torture displayed down there and I certainly was not looking forward to what might lie ahead. My fears were alleviated just slightly when a tiny, kind, very cheerful woman introduced herself as the physical therapist. She said, "Mr. Polson, we are going to restore you to a full range of motion in that arm. After all, motion is lotion!"

Well, it did not feel like lotion, but I certainly did experience a full range of *emotions*! As she continued to manipulate my arm, the therapist cheerfully said, "Today we are going to try for 15 to 20 degrees of movement, Mr. Polson." Within a few minutes, the room felt like 115 to 120 degrees Fahrenheit to me. The perspiration beaded on my forehead because the movement of my arm was so painful. As I recall, I accused that committed caregiver of being a *physical terrorist*!

As I look back on that experience today, I am grateful for that "painful" therapy because for over 25 years I have had that full range of motion in my left arm. It has not been stiff or limited in use at all. Physical therapy kept my arm from becoming immobilized and restricted in movement. Likewise, my friend, our Great Physician sometimes prescribes *spiritual therapy* so that rather than becoming immobilized or restricted by fear, we can know by experience his presence and his peace. The Lord wants us to know the *victory of peace over the virus of fear*.

God is the Great Physician. He is Jehovah-Rapha. *The Lord who heals*. And he will heal us of the virus of fear when we follow his prescribed therapy. In these verses from the Book of Philippians, God gives us *Therapy for Peace*. In the previous chapter, we considered his *Vaccine for Fear*, but God goes beyond just a vaccine. He gives us spiritual therapy that can produce and maintain his peace. Our Lord is the Prince of Peace, and he wants peace to *reign* in our hearts. His therapy regimen for this peace is clearly prescribed in the Book of Philippians. As we implement these therapeutic principles, they bring peace to strengthen us in the middle of whatever difficult situation we may be experiencing.

The first principle we must understand is that our Lord has promised the reality of his peace. Peace was the parting gift the Lord Jesus Christ promised to his disciples the night before his crucifixion.

> Peace I leave with you; **my peace I give to you**. Not as the world gives do I give to you. (John 14:27)

Notice Jesus said, "*my peace*," not "*your peace*." And notice further, Jesus said, "I *give* to you." This is not something we earn or achieve. It is a gift. Peace is a *grace gift* from the Prince of Peace, the Lord Jesus Christ. Now it is very important to remember that when Jesus promised peace for us, he was not guilty of partial disclosure or false advertising. Jesus was completely honest as he revealed to us something else about peace.

> "I have said these things to you, that in me you may have peace. In the world **you will have tribulation**. But take heart; I have overcome the world." (John 16:33)

Jesus said, "In the world *you will have tribulation*." Yes, there may be times when our trials are very unusually severe. In fact, there may be nothing we can compare them to that we have ever experienced before. Yes, our trials, at times, may be *unprecedented* but they should never be *unexpected* because Jesus predicted that our trials would come.

Our trials should never be unexpected.

Decades later, Peter, who was there that night and heard Jesus share those words, also reminded us that we should not be surprised by trials.

> Beloved, **do not be surprised** at the fiery trial when it comes upon you to test you, as though something strange were happening to you. (1 Pet. 4:12)

As followers of Christ, we should not consider it a strange thing when we go through trials. Trials for the people of God are normal, not abnormal

Paul, a veteran of trials, wrote this letter to the Philippians, thanking them for their prayerful and financial support. But, remember where Paul is located when he writes this letter to the Philippians. He is a prisoner in Rome. He is in jail...*again*. As you recall, Paul spent a lot of time in jail. In fact, it was in the jailhouse that the church of Philippi had its great beginning. Paul is in jail, again, but his attitude is the same as it was at midnight in that cell in Philippi years before, one of *jailhouse joy*.

> Even if I am to be poured out as a drink offering upon the sacrificial offering of your faith, I am glad and rejoice with you all. Likewise you also should be glad and rejoice with me. (Phil. 2:17-18)

That is so amazing. The authorities could imprison Paul but they could not imprison his spirit. Even though he was in chains, Paul was a free man because his spirit was free. He was filled with the joy and peace of the Lord Jesus Christ!

Paul writes to the Philippians who are also experiencing trials and mistreatment because of their faith. Their freedoms are being limited and infringed upon by the governmental authorities, and yet, what was Paul's message to them? Did he say, "You're being robbed of your civil liberties!" No. Paul said to them, "*You are being gifted with a sacred identity.*" In our trials, we should not consider ourselves being robbed of liberty, but rather being *gifted* with a sacred identity. What is that sacred identity?

> For it has been granted to you that for the sake of Christ you should not only believe in him but also **suffer for his sake**, (Phil. 1:29)

Paul tells the Philippians, and us as well, that suffering is a gift. Yes, a gift. With our gift of salvation has come another gift, and that is the gift of suffering for the sake of Christ. It is through suffering and following the Lord through that suffering, that we are granted a special identity, a shared identity with Jesus. We are privileged to identify ourselves with Christ when we suffer, and Paul says we should rejoice in that honor.

Paul had been in prison for over two years when he wrote these words. He was unjustly arrested in Jerusalem and put in prison in Caesarea. He was sent as a political prisoner on a vessel to Rome. He was shipwrecked after having saved the whole crew. Now, he is a prisoner in Rome awaiting trial before the emperor Nero. Having experienced all that injustice, it is important that we note what Paul *does not say*. He does not say, "*Pity me.*" Instead, he says, "*Rejoice with me.*" Paul is in prison but he is at peace. He is experiencing the promised reality of the Lord Jesus—the promised gift that Jesus gives in times of trials—the gift of peace.

The gift of peace is the *ultimate reality*. The Lord promises to each of us, as well, in our own times of trial—a piece of reality, and that is the reality of his peace. It is such a treasure that Paul, who is experiencing this peace, wants the Philippians to share in this peace as well. In fact, he wants *all believers of all time* to share in this peace. That is the reason the Holy Spirit inspired Paul to write this letter—so that believers through the ages when in deep trial, might share in the promised reality of God's peace in their hearts.

THE PERSONAL REGIMEN FOR PEACE

In Philippians, Chapter 4, Paul explains to us how we can experience this promised reality of peace. But, it is important to know that we are not neutral in this process. We do not just wait and then after waiting the Lord gives us peace. We *choose* to enter into the process, actively agreeing with the Lord, which produces his peace. Paul makes a promise about this in Philippians 4:7:

> And the peace of God, which surpasses all understanding, will **guard your hearts** and your minds in Christ Jesus.

Don't miss that intentional turn of the phrase which Paul uses. The peace of God will guard your hearts and minds. Then Paul says at the very end of Philippians 4:9, "...the God of peace will be with you."

> What you have learned and received and heard and seen in me—practice these things, and **the God of peace will be with you**.

The outcome of this regimen for peace is that the *peace of God* guards our hearts and minds and that peace comes from the *God of peace* who is with us. You see, peace is simply the manifested presence of the God of peace in our lives. This the result or outcome that Paul, by the Holy Spirit, wants us to experience.

Now, let's back up and examine the regimen that leads to the outcome of peace. What is it that leads to the peace of God guarding our hearts and minds, and the God of peace being with us? What is the regimen that leads to experiencing that reality? The regimen that leads to this outcome is based on three things that Paul mentions—*Our Attitude* (Phil. 4:2-7), *Our Attention* (Phil 4:8), and *Our Actions* (Phil. 4:9). Let's begin by focusing our attention on the first of these three essentials for peace—*Our Attitude*.

OUR ATTITUDE

Our attitude is incredibly important. Motivational speaker Zig Ziglar once declared, "It is your attitude...that will determine your altitude." Paul shares specifics about the attitude that we must have as believers to become people experiencing God's peace. In Philippians 4:2-7, Paul shares what I like to call his six "Be" attitudes that lead to peace.

PAUL'S "BE" ATTITUDES FOR PEACE

1. BE UNITED

As Paul outlines this timeless therapy for peace, he also shares a personal message to two members of the congregation in Philippi. Euodia and Syntyche are having a difficult time in maintaining a peaceful, personal relationship, so Paul speaks to them personally.

> **I entreat Euodia and I entreat Syntyche to agree in the Lord.** Yes, I ask you also, true companion, help these women, who have labored side by side with me in the gospel together with Clement and the rest of my fellow workers, whose names are in the book of life. (Phil. 4:2-3)

Can you imagine being one of those two ladies when the letter of Philippians was first read in the church of Philippi? My goodness, what a moment that must have been! Why did the Holy Spirit inspire Paul to address such a personal situation in this letter? Paul is prompted to do so because there is a lesson here for *all Christians, in all the church, for all the ages.* The lesson is this: we cannot expect to experience peace *within us* if there is no peace *between us.* Peace is not based on an acknowledgment of who is right or wrong; it is based on an acknowledgment of *who unites us.* We make the choice. We can choose to focus on our disagreements about many things (some of them even highlighted by this time of trial with the coronavirus), or we can choose to focus on the one who unites us and choose to be of one mind. How is this possible? Paul shares it is possible because of three words in verse two—"In the Lord." It is possible to be at peace when we can be of one mind *in the Lord*.

Peace requires *peacemaking* in the Lord, and it also requires *peacemakers*.

> Yes, I ask you also, true companion, help these women, who have labored side by side with me in the gospel together with Clement and the rest of my fellow workers, whose names are in the book of life. (Phil. 4:3)

Paul is speaking to someone who is a friend of Euodia and Syntyche. He pleads with this companion to help these women who have served and labored side-by-side with Paul and Clement. These are wonderful women of God. Their names are in the Book of Life. These are born-again ladies who need someone to come alongside them and help them to make peace with each other. They need a peacemaker. Being a peacemaker is directly connected with experiencing peace.

When we determine that we want to be peacemakers between others, we begin to bring peace into our own hearts and lives. Jesus said, "Blessed are the *peacemakers*." Part of being blessed is having joy and peace in our own hearts. And when we desire not to take sides in an argument but to unite people in the Lord, we are going to experience the benefits of that peace ourselves. Indeed, "Blessed are the peacemakers!"

The "Be" attitudes that lead to peace are first of all—*be united*. And secondly—*be joyful*.

2. BE JOYFUL

> "Rejoice in the Lord always; again I will say, rejoice." (Phil. 4:4)

The Apostle Paul literally *commands* us to be joyful. As a matter of fact, he commands us *twice*. "Rejoice in the Lord always; again I will say, rejoice," Paul makes such an emphasis on this subject because rejoicing in the Lord exalts Christ. Jesus is our joy, so when we choose to rejoice in him, we are exalting Christ. Joy exalts Jesus.

And then, there is another reason we are urged to rejoice. Rejoicing in the Lord *edifies ourselves*. We build up and strengthen the muscles of our faith when we choose to exercise our joy in him. Yes, rejoicing is a decision based on a determination we make to do it. Joy is not an emotion that is prompted by the circumstances from without. It is not the same as happiness, because the concept of *"happiness"* is connected to the *happenings* in our lives. Joy is rooted in that which is much deeper, spiritual, and eternal. Joy is the result of Jesus and his manifested presence in our lives. I remember, even now, over 50 years later the song we sometimes sang as children in our opening assemblies in Sunday school, "Joy is the flag flying high in the castle of my heart; for the King is in residence there." Yes, the King of Heaven resides in our hearts as believers. So, Paul tells us to exalt Christ, even in our trials. When we decide to exalt Christ by rejoicing in him, we edify ourselves.

3. BE GENTLE

> Let your reasonableness be known to everyone.
> (Phil 4:5)

The word Paul uses here for "reasonableness" is very unusual and almost untranslatable in English because so many subtleties of expression are included in it. Synonyms for the word include "forbearance," "generosity," "kindliness" or "mildness." Perhaps the best way to describe this word would be—*sweet reasonableness*. "Let your **sweet reasonableness** be known to all people." A person characterized by sweet reasonableness is kindly dispositioned toward others.

Strangely though, this kindness toward others is a gift that is hard to give away, because the people to whom you are being "sweetly kind" have a tendency to give it back. There is a great theological truth that we should be careful to grasp in our spiritual growth with the Lord—people generally treat us the way we treat them!

> **People generally treat us the way we treat them.**

When we practice sweet reasonableness, this virtue becomes its own reward. While scattering the seeds of kindness toward others we plant some of those seeds in our own hearts and eventually we reap the harvest of joy. Kindness is a gift that we give to others and also give to ourselves. For ultimately, the kindness we give is given back to us in return and our own spirits are enriched. Amazing. Grace always is.

4. BE EXPECTANT

> Let your [sweet] reasonableness be known to everyone. **The Lord is at hand** (Phil. 4:5).

Notice Paul says, "The Lord is at hand." This phrase can also be translated "the Lord is near." There is a difference of opinion among Bible scholars as to which meaning is emphasized in this verse, whether *the Lord is coming or the Lord is near or present*. The truth is that both meanings apply. This verse reminds us that the Lord is coming. No matter how difficult our day may be, it brings us one day closer to the coming of the Lord Jesus, or closer to going to be with him. Either way, we are one day closer to Jesus! And what a reason for joy that truly is!

Approximately, one out of every four verses in the New Testament refers to the second coming of Jesus Christ. That means twenty-five percent of the New Testament has some connection with Jesus' return. The second coming of Christ is at the very heart of what it means to be a Christian—to possess a confidant and expectant hope that Christ is indeed coming again. It is our blessed hope and it brings us joy. We must also remember that as we anticipate the Lord and his coming, it is also true that *the Lord is near*. "*Let your sweet reasonableness be known to everyone. The Lord is near.*" He is present. He is right here. Right now. We are not alone. My friend, whatever you are going through today, whatever you are experiencing—*you are not alone*. Even in the midst of any "social distancing" and isolation, you are not alone. The Lord is near. Rejoice!

5. BE PRAYERFUL

> Do not be anxious about anything, but in everything
> by prayer and supplication with thanksgiving let
> your requests be made known to God. (Phil. 4:6)

The next "Be" attitude involves prayer. Paul challenges us that because the Lord is near, we need to be prayerful. God is always close enough to hear our prayers.

I remember that my dad had a message plate attached to the front of his car that read, "Prayer changes things." In my mind's eye, I can see him driving down the road or pulling up at our house and that testimony being displayed on the front of the car, "Prayer changes things." Yes, prayer does indeed change things, and one thing prayer changes, according to Paul, is this: prayer changes worry into trust.

Prayer changes worry into trust.

"Don't worry" is Paul's challenge. "Don't be anxious about anything." The grammar Paul uses conveys the idea of stopping and starting. "*Stop being anxious about anything*," but "*start praying about everything.*" We could say it this way, "Stop worrying about anything and start praying about everything."

Worry robs us of life itself. The reason it is so terrible to live a life that is full of worry and anxiety is that this behavior robs us of our days. The original source of the following quote is unclear, but the truth it conveys is crystal clear, "*Remember, today is the tomorrow you worried about yesterday.*" We smile at that quip but the admonition should grip us. We can worry our life away one day at a time. Worry is toxic. Worry is poisonous. But, thank God, there is an antidote to worry that Paul prescribes—*prayer and supplication.*

"*Supplication*" means a specific request. In prayer with supplication, we take specific situations and issues to the Lord. We don't just generalize saying, "bless me" and "bless everyone." No, we ask the Lord for his help in very specific situations or needs regarding our lives or the lives of others.

As we pray and pour out our hearts to God in supplication, we must also remember something else Paul prescribes for our battle against the virus of fear—don't forget to *give thanks*. We certainly must give our problems to God, because prayer overcomes worry, but we must not forget to also lift our praise to God. We need to exalt our Master for who he is and what he has done for us, and what is ahead for us in Christ. As we take our praise to God and not just our problems, we will find that he will lead us to peace. "*In everything give thanks.*" Paul doesn't tell us to give thanks *for* everything but to give thanks *in* everything. We can give thanks even for things that are not pleasant.

I remember the story shared about the noted Bible commentator and minister of the 17th century, Matthew Henry, who was once robbed of his wallet. That night he read in his Bible the statement from verse 6, "In everything give thanks," and he wondered, "How can I give thanks about being robbed?" After a time of reflection and meditation, this is what he wrote in his journal:

> "Let me be thankful, first, because he never robbed me before; second, because although he took my purse, he did not take my life; third, because although he took all I possessed, it was not much; and fourth, because it was I who was robbed, not I who robbed."

In everything give thanks. Everything. Paul's "Be" attitudes are the restorative regimen for our souls: *be united, be joyful, be gentle, be expectant, be prayerful,* and finally:

6. BE PEACEFUL

> Do not be anxious about anything, but in everything by prayer and supplication with thanksgiving let your requests be made known to God. 7 **And the peace of God, which surpasses all understanding, will guard your hearts and your minds in Christ Jesus.** (Phil. 4:6-7)

Paul promises a supernatural peace, a peace that cannot be explained. It is a peace that surpasses understanding. This peace cannot *be explained*, but thank God, it can *be experienced.*

My friend, you can experience that peace today through the Prince of Peace, Jesus Christ.

> Therefore, since we have been justified by faith, we have **peace with God** through our Lord Jesus Christ. (Rom. 5:1)

Do you have peace with God? God has made peace with him possible, through the Peacemaker, Jesus Christ. When you trust in Jesus, repent of your sins, and place your faith in Christ, you are justified and declared not guilty by God. Then, the peace of God is made available to you. By God's grace and through faith, you can have *peace with God* right now which leads to the peace of God. This moment, turn away from anything else as your hope of peace, for it is a false hope that cannot provide lasting peace for your soul. But, the Prince of Peace, Jesus Christ, came to make peace between a holy God and helpless, hopeless sinners. He made that peace through the blood of his death on the cross as a sacrifice to God and a substitute for sinners. Through faith in what Jesus did for you on the cross, you can have the precious gift of peace. Once again, read this declaration and your invitation:

> Therefore, since we have been justified by faith, we
> have peace with God through our Lord Jesus Christ.
> (Rom. 5:1)

I pray that you will know that peace in your heart today—peace with God through Jesus Christ our Lord. May God also grant you today, as you follow this regimen from Philippians, Chapter 4, and in particular these "Be" attitudes, that you may experience the priceless outcome—*the peace of God which surpasses all understanding that will guard your heart and mind in Christ Jesus.*

PRAYER TO THE GOD OF PEACE

Lord, we thank you for this opportunity to open your Word and we pray as we come to the close of this chapter, that we may not become distracted in these sacred moments and quickly move on to other activities. Lord, may you draw us into your presence to respond to your marvelous grace. Heavenly Father, we are not sharing in God's Word together through this book by accident, but by appointment. And you, Great Physician, have a goal for each of us in this appointment, to experience peace with you through our Lord Jesus Christ—the unexplainable peace that surpasses all understanding. Oh Lord, I pray and ask that you will accomplish that purpose right now in the heart and mind of every reader. In Jesus' name.

Amen.

R.E.A.P. GUIDE

READ
- Philippians 4:4-9
- What lessons do you see the Holy Spirit teaching you in this text?

EXAMINE
- There is a way to reach the status that Paul says is available in verses 7 and 9, and it involves commands. As believers, we must remember that the commands of Chapter 4 have a context in the good news of the gospel. Look back at Philippians 3:20-4:1. How does Paul summarize the gospel hope we have and what does he tell us to do?
- What are the commands listed in verses 4-7? Are there any promises connected to them?

APPLY
- Stress, worry, concern, and anxiety result from a lack of peace. When in recent days have you experienced those symptoms of no peace? What kind of things cause you to experience those feelings?
- "Rejoice…again I will say, rejoice!" What do we have to rejoice about even in tough times?
- What types of things should we be thinking about and filling our minds within keeping with Paul's commands in verses 8-9?

PRAY
- Using the "PRAY" acronym, respond with **P**raise to the Lord, **R**epent of sins this Bible passage has revealed to you, **A**sk the Lord for any requests you have, and **Y**ield to his will.

- 7 -

THE GUARDIANS OF THE MIND

Finally, brothers, whatever is true, whatever is honorable, whatever is just, whatever is pure, whatever is lovely, whatever is commendable, if there is any excellence, if there is anything worthy of praise, think about these things. What you have learned and received and heard and seen in me—practice these things, and the God of peace will be with you.
(Phil. 4:8-9)

Max Lucado in his book, *The Applause of Heaven*, shares a very interesting story about the infamous robber of the 19th century known as Black Bart.

During his reign of terror between 1875 and 1883, he is credited with stealing the bags and the breath away from twenty-nine different stagecoach crews. And he did it all without firing a shot.

His weapon was his reputation. His ammunition was intimidation.

A hood hid his face. No victim ever saw him. No artist ever sketched his features. No sheriff could ever track his trail. He never fired a shot or took a hostage.

He didn't have to. His presence was enough to paralyze....

As it turns out he wasn't anything to be afraid of, either. When the hood came off, there was nothing to fear. When the authorities finally tracked down the thief, they didn't find a blood thirsty bandit from Death Valley; they found a mild-mannered druggist from Decatur, Illinois. The man the papers pictured storming through the mountains on horseback was, in reality, so afraid of horses he rode to and from his robberies in a buggy. He was Charles E. Boles--the bandit who never once fired a shot, because he never loaded his gun.

Black Bart paralyzed people by fear. Fear was his weapon and the ammunition was his reputation.

As believers, we have to be very careful that we don't let "Black Bart"—the virus of fear—get into our heads and rob our hearts. When fear gains entrance inside our minds, it takes control, and when fear takes control, it robs us. Yes, fear robs us of precious cargo that each one of us is carrying, or should be carrying, and that is the precious treasure of peace. Peace is a precious gift that our Lord Jesus Christ has given to us as his disciples.

> "Peace I leave with you; my peace I give to you. Not as the world gives do I give to you. Let not your hearts be troubled, neither let them be afraid." (John 14:27)

Peace in our hearts and minds is truly a grace gift from the Lord Jesus Christ. Our enemy, Satan, wants to rob us of this precious cargo we carry and he uses fear as his weapon to accomplish the crime. To keep from being victims of this pilfering of our peace, we must remove the hood from this bandit and determine that "Black Bart" has no authority to demand we give up anything that has been given to us by Jesus. His weapon of fear is full of blanks and we do not have to yield to him a single coin out of our treasure of peace. Philippians, Chapter 4, provides us with a manual on just how to do that.

The Apostle Paul is writing from prison but in his chains he is teaching us how to break free from the prison of fear. We can be *held captive by peace* instead. Regardless of what is going on around us, like Paul, we can live free from the virus of fear. Freedom begins in the mind, and in this passage, Paul challenges us to stop the *mind games* of fear by making sure that we do not let our minds become *playgrounds* for fear. Instead, we must turn our minds into *training camps for peace*.

In writing this manual, Paul maps out a three-fold regimen for peace of mind and heart. It requires *attitude, attention*, and *action*. First, we must uphold an *attitude of peace* (Phil. 4:2-7). Second, we must focus our *attention on peace* (Phil. 4:8), and third, we must engage our *actions for peace* (Phil. 4:9).

In the previous chapter, we focused on Paul's 6 great "Be" attitudes or qualities for peace. Let's review those quickly:

Be United (Phil. 4:2-3)
If we want to be people at peace, we must become peacemakers ourselves, helping others to be at peace.

Be Joyful (Phil. 4:4)
We are told to rejoice in the Lord. Apostle Paul commands us twice to be joyful in the Lord because he is the source of our joy.

Be Gentle (Phil. 4:5)
"Let your sweet reasonableness be known to all people." We must focus our dispositions toward gentleness, kindness, goodness, and forbearance.

Be Expectant (Phil. 4:5)
"The Lord is at hand" which has two implications: 1) *He is close by*, meaning we are not alone, and 2) *The Lord is coming*. No matter what is happening around us, the Lord is *near us*, and he is coming *for us*. This is one of the reasons we can be so joyful and live in a state of expectancy, knowing that the Lord Jesus Christ is both near and is coming soon. We have the security of his spiritual presence now and the confidence of his physical presence to come.

Be Prayerful (Phil. 4:6)
Paul challenges us to stop being anxious about anything and to start praying about everything. Paul, in effect, is saying, "Bring everything that causes disturbance in your heart to the Lord. Pray about it. Cast your burdens on the Lord. Take your life and all of its difficult circumstances to Christ, determining to stop allowing anxiety to have control of your mind."

Be Peaceful (Phil. 4:7)
Paul intentionally uses a startling contrast combining the promise of peace in military imagery. "*And the peace of God, which surpasses all understanding, will guard your hearts and your minds in Christ Jesus.*" As you read this, pay particular attention to this. Paul says,

"The peace of God will guard your hearts and minds…" What a powerful and unique image. The word for "guard" that is used here conveys the idea of a soldier on guard duty. The peace of God will "*stand guard*" around our minds.

The ultimate guardian of our minds is God, the Holy Spirit. The Bible tells us that the Holy Spirit begins his guard duty of our minds through the miracle of the new birth. He cleanses our depraved minds with the "washing of regeneration," as Paul describes it in Titus 3:4-5:

> But when the goodness and loving kindness of God our Savior appeared, he saved us, not because of works done by us in righteousness, but according to his own mercy, by the washing of **regeneration** and renewal of the Holy Spirit. (Titus 3:4-5)

As believers, we have been subjected to brainwashing, and we should praise God for this because our minds are desperately dirty. We have been brainwashed by the washing of regeneration through the renewing work of the Holy Spirit. He is now the Great Guardian of our minds. Our minds are also guarded through the ministry of the Captain of our Salvation, Jesus Christ. In 1 Corinthians 2:16, Paul shares that as believers we now have the mind of Christ through the regeneration of the Holy Spirit. When we were born again by faith, this renewing work began. Our minds, which were once deprived and darkened in sin, have been made new by the miracle of regeneration. As believers, we have been given minds alive to Christ and we can now think God's thoughts through him.

> "For who has understood the mind of the Lord so as to instruct him?" But we have the mind of Christ. (1 Cor. 2:16)

This "mind of Lord" has been granted to us because of our *position* in Christ, but we must put this mind into *practice*. Earlier in this letter to the Christian Philippians, Paul said, "Have this mind among yourselves, which is yours in Christ Jesus..." (Phil. 2:5) "Let" is a word of agreement. By cooperating with him, Jesus Christ functions as the Captain of the Guard of our minds. We as soldiers of Christ are also participants in the process of guarding our minds. We have the responsibility to stand at attention, as it were, and stay alert. We must be attentive to our thought life and therefore cannot allow our thoughts to just wander unchallenged wherever they want. Paul, by the Holy Spirit, is calling us on guard duty to protect our thinking and to be mentally alert. There is no time for "chilling out on vacation," so to speak. We must be fully engaged, guarding our thoughts with mental attention.

So, if we are called to attention in guarding our thoughts, what is it that we are supposed to be *attentive* to? Paul answers that question in verse 7 when he tells us to guard our "hearts and minds." These two words, "heart" and "mind," are synonyms but they are not identical. They are synonyms for our inner nature or the spiritual aspect of our being. The "mind" has to do with our volition, or how we *think*. Our "heart" has to do more with our emotions—what we *feel* or what we *sense*. Paul is referring to what we often call our *consciousness*. His challenge then, and that of the Holy Spirit, is for us to stand guard over our hearts and our minds. We must protect both our emotional consciousness and our volitional consciousness in order to maintain the peace of God that resides within us.

This call to mentally stand guard and protect the peace of God leads us to an important question. What specifically are we to stand guard against? The Scripture is very clear in answering that question with repeated warnings about three infiltrators that want to creep into the camp of our thinking, creating turmoil and robbing us of God's peace. The three members of this squad are *the world, the flesh,* and *the devil.*

These three enemies desire to slink into our thinking and overcome our peace by transferring our focus onto things that are not of the Lord. *The flesh* in the Bible refers to the remaining influence of sin that is still present within us as sinful, not yet fully redeemed, human beings. Our peace can be overtaken when we focus on those things which are part of our old pattern of mental processes. This traitorous infiltrator of the flesh is already within us. *The world* refers to the values and vanities of the world system that exists on this planet in rebellion to the Creator. And then there is the devil, the archenemy of *God* and God's image-bearers. *The devil* desires to capture our allegiance through focusing our attention on that which is not of the truth and therefore not of God. *The world, the flesh,* and *the devil*—we have to stand on guard against these three infiltrators. They are so deceptive and so very gifted at impersonating our allies, but they are robbers of our peace in the Lord.

THE PASSWORDS OF PEACE

So, here is the huge question: how can we possibly defend the gateways to our minds against these infiltrators of our peace? The answer is we can keep our minds safe only by challenging our thoughts with the *passwords of peace*. The Captain of our Salvation has provided us with inspired words to guard the gates of our minds. These passwords identify our thoughts as either *friendly* to our well-being or *threats* to our well-being. It is our duty to test our thoughts by using these passwords of peace that Paul shares with us from Philippians 4:8.

> Finally, brothers, whatever is **true**, whatever is **honorable**, whatever is **just**, whatever is **pure**, whatever is **lovely**, whatever is **commendable**, if there is any **excellence**, if there is anything **worthy of praise**, think about these things. (Phil. 4:8)

TRUE

Paul challenges us to think about those things that are true. He is not referring only to those things that are *factually* true, but those things that are *faithfully* true. *Faithfully true* encompasses all those things that are in agreement with the truth of God. We are not to focus our thoughts on things just because they are *factually* true. In this fallen world, that could include many factually true topics or issues that would not be edifying to our hearts and minds. The question to ask is this— are these things *faithfully* true? Do these thoughts agree with the truth of God?

HONORABLE

Another password of peace is focusing our thoughts on those things that are honorable. Honorable means *noble* or *respectful*. The Greeks and Romans highly valued this quality of mind which characterized a person who communicated a manner of dignity and disposition. Honorable thinking rises above a focus on concepts that cheapen and devalue life. This level of thinking is not worthy of those created in God's image.

JUST

As followers of Christ, we are to focus our thoughts on those things that are *just*. The word Paul uses here means *righteous*. So, his challenge is to focus our thoughts on that which is *in harmony and agreement with God's character*. We are to reject thinking patterns that do not reflect the character of God because they are by nature *ungodly*.

PURE

We are to focus our thoughts on pure things as well. Thoughts that are pure are *morally clean*, meaning they are not dirty or filthy. So much of today's media is comparable to a sewer flowing with filth. It is almost impossible to escape the stench of it, but that does not mean we have to allow our minds to become a septic tank. By God's grace, we can choose to think on the things in life that are morally clean.

LOVELY

Think on the things that are *lovely*. The word lovely is unique. In fact, this is the only time this word appears in the New Testament. The primary concept of the word is *attractive*, but it means attractive in the sense that it *prompts love*; it draws love out of the heart. Thinking on things that are lovely or attractive will focus our attention on ideas or objects that draw out the highest qualities within us.

COMMENDABLE

We are also to think on things which are *commendable*. Something that is commendable is *highly respected* or *well-thought of*. Paul is challenging us to set our minds on those things that are admirable and not to settle for a mindset that is satisfied with "average" as its highest goal. We cannot fulfill our Lord's calling to be "the light of the world" with thinking that is common and dull.

EXCELLENT & PRAISE WORTHY

Paul could have continued with a lengthy list of qualities for virtuous thinking, but instead, he summarizes other qualities that could join these "guardians of our mind" by commending to us subjects and concepts that are excellent and praiseworthy. *Excellent* means possessing the quality of *intrinsic value*. And then, Paul encourages us to think on anything that is *worthy of praise*, meaning anything that is well spoken of and *deserves to be well spoken of*. Finally, the word Paul uses in his challenge to "think" on these qualities is very important. It is a word that denotes a mind that is *actively engaged* on a subject or object. Perhaps it might be helpful to paraphrase Paul's challenge to us as "*concentrate on these things.*" He is serious about what our minds focus upon and wants us to get serious as well. Why would Paul go to such lengths to be so *descriptive* and *prescriptive* about our thought life? Why is he calling us to such attentiveness in standing guard on our thought-life? It is because Paul knows what we all really must know—*our thoughts are the key to our identity.*

It has been well said by insightful people, "You may not be what you think you are, but what you THINK, you ARE."

You are what you think.

Our thinking process ultimately is expressed in our living process. How we live is always the outworking of how we think. Our thinking is the key to our identity. What Paul has shared in these verses is the wisdom of God communicated by so many of his servants through the ages. In fact, the wisest man who ever lived wrote these words of challenge about guarding our thought-life:

> Keep your heart with all vigilance, for from it flow the springs of life. (Prov. 4:23)

Many people protest this by saying, "Well, we can't help what we think about. That's impossible." Well, of course we can help what we think about! How do we know this? *Because God says we can.* God promises us that by the power of the Holy Spirit we can *determine* what we think about. Through the inspiration of the Spirit, Paul shares with us in this passage the regimen to bring our thoughts under control. In fact, he promises that we can do more than just control our thoughts. We can actually renew our thinking processes by actively engaging our minds in these qualities that guard our peace.

The key to implementing this renewal of our minds is not by focusing on individual thoughts, but rather to focus on the direction of our thinking. Paul is not saying that we are never going to have a bad thought, but he is saying that we don't have to let our minds be *controlled* by those thoughts.

Martin Luther, the great reformer, quipped, "You cannot keep birds from flying over your head, but you can keep them from building a nest in your hair." Yes, we certainly have bad thoughts from time to time, in fact, often. However, Paul is challenging us to create a *renewed environment* in our minds that no longer welcomes destructive thought-processes fueled by the world, the flesh, and the devil. We must determine that because we really are *new* people in Jesus Christ, our minds will no longer be "home" for our *old* ways of thinking.

Many years ago, a woman came to me for some counseling regarding her marriage. I was somewhat surprised because she had not been married that long. She had married later in life to a man who was a widower. As I talked with her and asked her to share with me what was happening, she said, "Pastor, I love him and I believe he loves me, but I'm really struggling." I asked her to please help me to try to understand the difficulty and she said, "Well, we were married last year and then I moved into his house. But Pastor, there are pictures of his former wife everywhere, all over the house, and it is so troubling to me!"

A few days later I met with her husband and I explained his wife's concern. I said to him, "Brother, do you remember that beautiful service you had for your first wife in the funeral home?"

He said, "Yes, certainly I remember that."

I continued, "My brother, you have got to have a funeral service like that *in your home*. Your first wife will always have a special place in your heart but she cannot continue to live in your home. There is only room for you and your new wife in your home."

The Lord gave that man understanding about the placement of priority his present wife deserved, and he responded to her with such grace and encouragement. A great peace came into their marriage as a change of focus came to the photographs in their home!

Likewise, if we are going to have thoughts that follow the Lord's will, they must be thoughts of our new life in Jesus Christ. And how beautiful that life is!

> Finally, brothers, whatever is **true**, whatever is **honorable**, whatever is **just**, whatever is **pure**, whatever is **lovely**, whatever is **commendable**, if there is any **excellence**, if there is anything **worthy of praise**, think about these things. (Phil. 4:8)

Paul reminds us that there is beauty *all around us*. Those things should be the controlling focus *within us*.

THE BEAUTY IN GOD'S WORLD

We understand that this world is broken, sinful, and fallen, and there are many dark and evil qualities that can be seen, felt, and experienced here. But beauty still exists. There is so much in this world that is true, honorable, just, pure, lovely, commendable, excellent, and worthy of praise. These qualities that Paul mentions here were commended by pagans, not just believers. There is much in this world that is worthy of our focus and commendation. Paul said, "Think on those things. Think on the beautiful things in this world."

THE BEAUTY IN THE WORD OF GOD

There exists for us another source of beauty. We can think on the beautiful things that are in the *Word* of God. The Word of God is *true*. The Word of God is *honorable*. The Word of God is *just*. The Word of God is *pure*. The Word of God is *lovely*.

The Word of God is *commendable*. The Word of God is *excellent*. The Word of God is *worthy of praise*. We find these qualities *in* the Word, so we need to fill our minds *with* the Word of God.

THE BEAUTY IN GOD'S WONDERFUL SON

And where else do we see beauty? We see beauty in God's world, we see beauty in God's Word, but we also see beauty in God's wonderful Son, Jesus. What we have been given in Philippians 4:8 is a portrait of Jesus! When we focus on Jesus what do we discover about him? We are continually delighted to see that Jesus is true, Jesus is *honorable*, Jesus is *just*, Jesus is *pure*, Jesus is *lovely*, Jesus is *commendable*, Jesus is *excellent*, and Jesus is so, so very *worthy of praise*.

We protect our treasure of peace by focusing our thinking on beauty—the things that are beautiful in God's world, in God's Word, and in God's wonderful Son, Jesus. We guard our minds by actively thinking on these gifts from our Heavenly Father.

Finally, there is one final aspect of Paul's prescribed regimen for peace. Along with maintaining the right *attitude* and the right *attention*, we must also *take the right action*. Paul challenged those first-century believers and he challenges us today with the same admonition:

> What you have learned and received and heard and seen in me—practice these things, and the God of peace will be with you. (Phil. 4:9)

If we desire to be people who overcome the virus of fear, then we must be people of action. And the right action is to put into practice those things that we have *learned* and have *received*. Learning and receiving must always travel together on the journey of spiritual growth. The word "learned" is connected to the same term that is translated "*disciple.*" Paul is calling the

Philippians to remember the things he shared with them in the process of their discipleship. The word "received" has to do with the *body of truth* that they received—the teachings of Jesus and the applications of the message of the gospel.

Then in a very personal manner, Paul reminds them of what they had actually heard from him personally in those precious days they shared together. He reminds them of all the moments that he was investing his life into theirs. They did not just *hear* him teach; they *saw* him walk out those teachings. Paul had communicated more than just a message to them; he also modeled a way of life. He challenged these believers not only to remember his words but to also follow his ways. Humbly, he could honestly say to them, "The things that you learned from me as I discipled you, the things that I communicated to you, the Word of the Gospel, the message of Christ, the things that you have heard and seen in my manner of living—*you do these things*, and the God of peace will be with you."

Peace is the manifested presence of the God of peace.

MODELS OF PEACE

If we are going to experience peace then we need to follow role models of peace. Who are your role models? Some of us have no peace because the people that we model our lives after are not peace-filled people. Paul was a peace-filled man. He was filled with the Spirit of God, the Word of God, and the love of God. In an environment of almost constant opposition and persecution, Paul was a man characterized by peace. Even from prison, he could joyfully and confidently say, "Now, you follow me as I follow Christ, and you will know peace." This call from Paul is so much more than a command; it is an invitation to experience God. He promised, "The God of peace will be with you." One of the results of a wasted life is the absence of peace. "The way of peace they have not known" (Isa. 59:8) is the tragic commentary on the self-directed life of those who do not follow the Lord. Peace is not something we achieve; it is a gift of God himself. Peace is the manifested presence of the God of peace. To live without peace is to live without God. Without a doubt, that is the greatest of all robberies! And sadly, it is a robbery in which people victimize themselves because the Lord offers himself and his peace to all as a free gift.

God offers this ultimate and complete peace to you today, my friend. The gift of his peace can be yours. "Therefore, since we have been justified by faith, we have peace with God through our Lord Jesus Christ" (Rom. 5:1-3). Peace *with* God was made by Jesus and the *peace of God* will be *guarded* in your life by Jesus. "And the peace of God, which surpasses all understanding, will guard your hearts and minds in Christ Jesus" (Phil. 4:7). The Prince of Peace is calling today: "Peace I leave with you; my peace I give to you. Not as the world gives do I give to you. Let not your hearts be troubled, neither let them be afraid" (John 14:27).

PRAYER

Almighty Lord, thank you for being the God of peace and for making peace with us, rebellious sinners, through the sacrifice of your precious Son. Thank you, that being justified through faith we have peace with God through our Lord Jesus Christ. May the Prince of Peace rule and reign as Captain of our souls. Help us to stand guard over this gift of peace that you have so graciously given us. May we not allow the virus of fear to contaminate our minds, robbing us of that peace which Jesus won through his great victory. Because of his victory, help us to choose joy today. Yes, may we rejoice in the Lord who is forever worthy of our praise. In his mighty and victorious name, we pray.

Amen.

R.E.A.P. GUIDE

READ
- Philippians 4:8-9
- What lessons do you see the Holy Spirit teaching you in this text?

EXAMINE
- The Apostle Paul has been speaking in Philippians 4:8-9 about one main spiritual reality God wants each of his people to have. What is that reality according to verse 9?
- How would you summarize the responsibility Paul says believers have, in verses 8-9, to live in this spiritual reality?

APPLY
- What types of things should we be thinking about and filling our minds within keeping with Paul's commands in verses 8-9?
- These qualities Paul lists are most evident in the life of Jesus Christ. What can you recall about the Lord that helps you better meditate on these qualities?

PRAY
- Using the "PRAY" acronym, respond with **P**raise to the Lord, **R**epent of sins this Bible passage has revealed to you, **A**sk the Lord for any requests you have, and **Y**ield to his will.

- 8 -

SHELTERED IN GOD

He who dwells in the shelter of the Most High
will abide in the shadow of the Almighty.
I will say to the Lord, "My refuge and my
fortress, my God, in whom I trust."
For he will deliver you from the snare of the
fowler and from the deadly pestilence.
He will cover you with his pinions,
and under his wings you will find refuge;
his faithfulness is a shield and buckler.
You will not fear the terror of the night,
nor the arrow that flies by day,
nor the pestilence that stalks in darkness,
nor the destruction that wastes at noonday.
A thousand may fall at your side,
ten thousand at your right hand,
but it will not come near you.
You will only look with your eyes
and see the recompense of the wicked.

*Because you have made the Lord your dwelling
place—the Most High, who is my refuge—
no evil shall be allowed to befall you,
no plague come near your tent.
For he will command his angels concerning you
to guard you in all your ways.
On their hands they will bear you up,
lest you strike your foot against a stone.
You will tread on the lion and the adder;
the young lion and the serpent you will
trample underfoot.
"Because he holds fast to me in love, I will
deliver him; I will protect him, because he
knows my name.
When he calls to me, I will answer him;
I will be with him in trouble;
I will rescue him and honor him.
With long life I will satisfy him
and show him my salvation."*
(Ps. 91:1-16)

I recently read an article about billionaire David Geffen who for many years has been involved in the production of several noteworthy films as part of "DreamWorks SKG." SKG stands for Steven Spielberg, Jeffrey Katzenberg, and David Geffen. On March 28 of 2020, in the middle of the coronavirus epidemic, Mr. Geffen personally produced a picture that was only shown for one day. It was not a film but a photograph of his 550 million dollar luxury superyacht anchored in the Caribbean near the Grenadine Island chain.

Mr. Geffen posted on Instagram a photo of a sunset with its fading golden beams of light shimmering behind his beautiful, 550-million-dollar vessel. Geffen's post on Instagram read, "Sunset, last night...isolated in the Grenadines avoiding the virus..."

You could almost hear the huge public groan in response saying, *"Really? That's the message you're sending out? Isolating from the virus on your 550-million-dollar yacht at sunset in the Grenadine Islands of the Caribbean?!"* As I said, the post did not stay up very long.

Most of us were experiencing a little different kind of "sheltering." Regardless, whether sheltered on a 550-million-dollar yacht or sheltered at home, however humble that might be, there exists a virus that can creep into and infect any residence and that is the virus of fear.

The pandemic of fear is ancient, universal, and truly deadly. But, thank God, there exists a vaccine that is completely effective and completely free. Once again, let us turn to someone who knew what it meant to be deeply infected by the virus of fear, but also experienced a vaccination that turned his worry into worship. On many occasions, our friend David struggled deeply with fear in his life, but he also experienced the sufficiency of God that so filled his heart with joy-filled confidence, he had to write a song of praise about it. The song that David wrote regarding the victory over fear was inspired by God and included in our Bibles as Psalm 91—one of the most beloved Psalms of David.

PSALM 91

The key to this passage is found in verse 5 when David says,

> **You will not fear** the terror of the night, nor the arrow that flies by day,

This Psalm is amazing in so many ways. The depth of it we could not begin to cover in an entire book, let alone one chapter. Psalm 91 is filled with meditations from the shepherd-king, David, to nourish the souls of God's sheep throughout their journey home. It is a song of shelter. In fact, it is a song of "sheltering at home" in safety from fear. What makes this song so unusual and so beautiful is that God himself is celebrated as the believer's ultimate shelter.

THE PERSONAL RESIDENCE FOR GOD'S PEOPLE
(Psalm 91:1-2)

In verses 1-2, notice how David describes the personal place of residence and shelter for the people of God.

> He who dwells in the shelter of the Most High will abide in the shadow of the Almighty. I will say to the Lord, "My refuge and my fortress, my God, in whom I trust." (Ps. 91:1-2)

The setting for this song is in the Judaean wilderness, and it is truly a wilderness, a region that receives very little rainfall and is almost devoid of any vegetation. It is incredibly hot during the day and frigid at night. This is the place David had to consider as his home for lengthy periods of time, especially when he was fleeing for his life from King Saul. Again, no vegetation, very little water, and burning heat, but David finds shelter in this Judaean wilderness. In the deep canyons formed by the steep barren cliffs, David and his men found that the shadows provided them wonderful shelter from the elements and the relentless spies of King Saul.

Anyone who has ever been in a very arid climate and felt the burning rays of the sun knows the immediate relief that is experienced when stepping into any available shade. David and his men experienced that relief. They also found safety in the shadows formed by the barren rocks, because the brightness of the sunlight and the barrenness of the landscape afforded no cover from their many enemies. Going into those canyons formed by the steep cliffs, David found, not just shadows, but a home in which he came to consider his refuge and his fortress.

The cooling shadows brought David *physical* rest as well as *emotional* rest for his soul, but there in the wilderness, he also found *spiritual* rest. While hiding in those canyons and shadows, David recognized that they were only a *physical expression* of his *ultimate* place of safety, shelter, and refuge which was really God himself.

That is the reason David writes this beautiful Psalm. By God's grace, he begins to see his circumstances and his surroundings in a very different light. They remind him of his supreme place of safety and shelter—the Lord his God.

David's place of hiding became a place of worship.

In verse 2 David gives voice to his choice of praise, "I will say to the Lord, 'My refuge and my fortress, my God, in whom I trust.'" We are permitted to listen to the working of David's thoughts of worship, "God, it is not these canyons that are my shelter. *You are my shelter.* You are my dwelling place. You are the place of safety for me. You are for me an unimaginable residence." Yes, David is living in a safe place, in the safety of his God.

Dear friend, I want you to know that God is still that place of shelter. The God that we worship, the God of David, is shelter indeed. He is still the refuge. He is still the fortress. He is still the same God. But who are the people who are able to experience God's shelter as David did three thousand years ago? There is a very clear answer to that question. The people who are able to experience God's refuge are those who **trust**. It is very important to unite that concept of "trust" in verse 2 with what David has just shared in the opening line of his song. "He who **dwells** in the shelter of the Most High..." In your Bible, circle that word "dwell" and connected it to the word in verse two—"trust." Who is the one who dwells in the shadow of the Almighty? Who is the one who can say, "God is my refuge?" It is the person who **trusts** in the Lord and who has an unqualified reliance on God. People who trust God experience God as their place of shelter. It is the reality of God that is only experienced by *faith*. Faith is the substance of our souls that connects us with the ultimate reality of our living God. And this is exactly where David takes us in his song, into the reality of God himself.

THE POWERFUL REALITIES FOR GOD'S PEOPLE
(Psalm 91:3-13)

Notice in verses 3 through 13, as David is sharing about the beautiful and powerful realities available for God's people, he is sharing about his "dwelling place," his "shelter," his "refuge" and his "fortress." These are all descriptions of his personal residence where he lives, sheltered in the Almighty. God, his refuge; God, his dwelling place. But, even as David goes out into the activities and inevitable challenges of life, God is still his reality. And so, beginning in verse 3 through verse 13, David promises that the daily reality of God he has personally experienced is available to God's people, regardless of what any day may bring. The daily reality of God is for all who trust in him. God is *that* real. God is not wishful thinking; God *is* reality.

The word David uses eight times to express the promise of God's living reality is the word—*will*. David says in verse 3, "He *will* deliver you." In verse 4, "He *will* cover you." In verse 5, "You *will* not fear." In verse 7, "It *will* not come near you." In verse 8, "You *will* only look with your eyes and see the recompense of the wicked." Verse 11, "He *will* command his angels to watch over you." In verse 12, "They *will* bear you up." Then in verse 13, "You *will* tread on the lion and on the adder..." These are promises of God's reality. These verses truly share *the will* of God.

Then, notice *two amazing images* of how real God is to David. I hope these images rest on your heart as you continue to meditate on Psalm 91. Notice the images that God inspires David to use regarding the reality of God to his people. First, God uses the image of a *mother bird,* and then he uses the image of a *military battle*. The image of a mother bird is one of the most beautiful passages in all of the Psalms of David:

> For he will deliver you from the snare of the fowler
>   and from the deadly pestilence.
> He will cover you with his pinions,
>   and under his wings you will find refuge;
>   his faithfulness is a shield and buckler.
> (Ps. 91:3-4)

What a sweet and tender, and yet, startling image. It is an image that no one would dare use for Almighty God unless God himself had inspired David to make use of it. It is the image of God Almighty covering his people like a *mother bird* would cover her chicks. This is the image of the Lord God spreading himself out over his people...an image of absolute love. It conveys a love so great that it is willing to sacrifice, even to the point of death.

My friend, that is exactly what God did. He loved that much. God *so loved* the world through the outstretched arms of his Son, Jesus Christ. Jesus used this image of the mother bird, evoked by David, as he was riding into Jerusalem on the day we now call Palm Sunday. People were shouting, "Hosanna to the Son of David; blessed is the he who comes in the name of the Lord; hosanna in the highest" (Matt. 21:9). The Bible says that Jesus in the midst of that praise was weeping and crying out,

> "O Jerusalem, Jerusalem, the city that kills the
> prophets and stones those who are sent to it! How
> often would I have gathered your children together as
> a hen gathers her brood under her wings, and you
> were not willing!" (Luke 13:34)

Five days later, Jesus did spread himself out over his people. The Bible tells us that though Jesus was rejected as the rightful King, yet he went to the cross wearing a crown. Yes, the crowned one on the cross with his arms outstretched in love, covered his people with the sacrifice of his own body and his blood. He spread himself in substitution and sacrifice and absorbed the wrath due to sinners—giving his life that we might live. This is the God we serve. A God that is so loving, so tender, and so very kind that he came to this earth and spread himself out, taking upon himself the judgment *our sins deserved*. What a God we serve! How precious he is!

That God is our same God today and he cares for us with a love that is beyond imagination. Under his wings, there is no fear.

Under God's wings, there is no fear.

In this shelter of the Almighty, the shadow beneath the cross-centered love of God, there is absolutely no fear. No virus can reach us there.

Now notice one other image that David uses in this beautiful song—the image of a military conflict or battle. This God who loves us with such tenderness is also going to be with us in the midst of battle! David says in verse 4 that the Lord will be "a shield and buckler." Then, in verse 5 & 6 he promises,

> You will not fear the terror of the night, nor the arrow that flies by day, nor the pestilence that stalks in darkness, nor the destruction that wastes at noonday.

David continues with the imagery of warfare in verse 7:

> A thousand may fall at your side,
> ten thousand at your right hand,
> but it will not come near you.
> (Ps. 91:7)

Again, these are graphic images of battle, but in the midst of the battle, God's chosen ones are secure. And then, as if these promises were not enough in describing God's protection of his people, David declares that heavenly angels are assigned to us to help us during our time of struggle here on earth:

> For he will command his angels concerning you
>   to guard you in all your ways.
> On their hands they will bear you up,
>   lest you strike your foot against a stone.
> (Ps. 91:11-12)

Hebrews 1:14 speaks in the same way regarding these angels who are our unseen guardians:

> Are they not all ministering spirits sent out to serve
> for the sake of those who are to inherit salvation?
> (Heb. 1:14)

The angels are "ministering spirits" that have been sent forth to serve us, those who will be the heirs of salvation. When we are in times of deepest trials, we are not alone. The Holy Spirit is with us, along with angels that have been assigned for our care to provide for us and protect us. We are often in the midst of spiritual and physical struggles and conflict, but indwelt by the Spirit of God, we are upheld by the angels of God. No wonder David can assure us, "You will not fear!" (Ps. 91:5)

Concerning this passage in Psalm 91, I recall something that Tim Keller, the pastor of Redeemer Presbyterian Church in New York City said during a session at a ministry conference. He specifically referred to verses 11 and 12 in his address entitled, "Satanic Exposition." What a title! He called it "Satanic Exposition" because this is the very passage that Satan quoted as he tempted the Lord Jesus Christ to cast himself down from the pinnacle of the temple if he were the Son of God.

Yes, Satan uses Scripture! What was Satan trying to do? He was trying to keep Jesus from fulfilling the will of God. He was trying to tempt Jesus into trusting *in his own way* rather than committing himself fully to *the will of God*. In effect, Satan was saying this, "You don't have to suffer, Jesus. There is another way that you can still do the will of God without suffering."

Satan knows how to take Scripture out of context and twist it. The Lord Jesus Christ trusted completely in God. He knew that his Father's will was the way of salvation and he committed himself even to the point of unimaginable suffering. It is passages like these and others that are also twisted in the name of so-called "Christianity" saying that if we have enough faith then we don't have to suffer. We are told that we can create our own reality and when we speak the words of faith it will be done. I trust you know that this is completely contrary to the Word of God and such blasphemous teaching. The Lord Jesus himself was called to suffer in order to accomplish God's purposes of salvation and the Bible says that we are also called to *follow in his steps*. We are called to suffer at times. In fact, we often suffer not because we are *out* of the will of God, but in truth, we will suffer because we are *in* the will of God.

God has ordained that in our suffering and our trial, we will know him as our dwelling place, our shelter, our refuge, our strength, and our fortress. That, my friend, is *Spirit-directed exposition* that the Lord wants us to apply to our hearts.

Finally, notice the promises that the Lord gives through this song of David in the closing phrases of God's praise. David sings about the *promised rewards* for the Lord's people. Yes, there is the reality of suffering and struggle, but God will reward us. Even though it will be difficult, the difficulties will seem like nothing compared to the overwhelming privileges which our God will make known to us.

ALREADY, BUT NOT YET

We live in what the teachers of the Reformation often designated as the *"already-not yet"* season of our salvation. We are already delivered, but not yet completely delivered. We are already healed, but not yet completely healed. We are already children of Heaven, but we are not yet in Heaven. We are already God's glorified ones, but we are not yet glorified in his presence. This is the existence we live in as we make our journey home—a*lready, but not yet.*

THE PROMISED REWARDS FOR GOD'S PEOPLE
(Ps. 91:14-16)

My friend, the promises of God are absolutely certain. There is the present reality of God and his love for us. There is the present reality of his protection, but he has promised rewards for his people. God speaks through David regarding these promises in verses 14 through 16:

> "Because he holds fast to me in love, I will deliver him;
> I will protect him, because he knows my name.
>
> When he calls to me, I will answer him;
> I will be with him in trouble;
> I will rescue him and honor him.
>
> With long life I will satisfy him
> and show him my salvation."

In these verses, three great rewards are promised by the Lord for those who have him as their dwelling place, for those who find their shelter in him as their home. First of all, God promises that he will hold us.

God will "hold" us.

Verse 14, "Because he holds fast to me in love, I will deliver him; I will protect him because he knows my name." You see, when we are holding fast to the Lord, in reality, *he is holding fast to us*. Our response in taking hold of him is because he has taken hold of us. We hold him and he holds us. That is the union that we have in Christ. And the Lord promises we will be held by him. He will hold us fast. We will not be lost. We will not be allowed to drift away. We are held by him because we have come to know his name. What does that mean to *"know his name?"* It means that we know him for who he really is by living experience. We do not just know *about* him, we *know him*. We are held to him by a loving union that is eternal life itself.

God will "hear" us.

The second reward that God promises to those who reside by faith in him is that *he will hear us*.

> When he calls to me, I will answer him;
> I will be with him in trouble;
> I will rescue him and honor him.
> (Ps. 91:15)

Notice, "when he calls...I will answer." That is a promise from God, that in times of trouble he is "a very present help in time of need." (Ps. 46:1). The Lord is not distant, "The Lord is at hand" as Paul shares in Philippians 4:5. When we call, he is listening because we are his children and he cares for us so tenderly. When we call, he listens. One of the great and priceless rewards for the people of God is that our God is also our Heavenly Father whose ear is always attentive to the voices of his dear children. When we call upon the Lord in times of trouble, we can be rest assured that he will hear us.

The final reward the Lord promises to us in this beautiful song is that as we make him our refuge and fortress, he will graciously honor us. How amazing is our Lord that gives us himself as our home, but also gives us honor!

> "With long life I will satisfy him and show him my salvation." (Ps. 91:16)

Now someone might say, *"How can it be that the Lord gives long-life to people who trust in him, who believe in him, and hold to him as their dwelling place when there are so many Christians who don't live a long life? They are taken from us early in life?"* What is the answer to that? The answer is this—the length of a person's life is not measured in the *quantity* of days; it is measured in the *quality* of days. For a Christian, there is no limit to their days because to be absent from the body is to be present with the Lord. (2 Cor. 5:8) The Bible says that we have eternal life and that one day we will go to be with the Lord and it will be an eternal day, a day without end, worshiping in his presence.

We *do* have a *quantity* of days! But on this planet earth, what matters most is that in the quantity of days that the Lord gives to us, there is a *quality* of life. The Lord promised abundant life. Jesus said, "I came that they may have life and have it abundantly" (John 10:10). That is his promise of quantity and quality of days, life forever, but also the promise of life right now. Being a Christian does not just mean there is life after death. To be a Christian means there is life *before and after death*. We have real-life now and we will have incredible everlasting life in the presence of the Lord one day, a day which will last forever.

What is life? Have you ever asked yourself that question? *What is life?* Is it just a succession of days? In the Bible, Jesus tells us what life really is. When praying in the Garden of Gethsemane, Jesus said this to his Father:

> And this is eternal life, **that they know you**, the only true God, and Jesus Christ whom you have sent. I glorified you on earth, having accomplished the work that you gave me to do. (John 17:3-4)

What is eternal life? "*...that they might know you, the only true God, and Jesus Christ whom you have sent.*" That, my friend, is eternal life. Eternal life is knowing God, knowing him personally through his Son Jesus Christ whom he has sent. That is *eternal life* and also true *life*.

The Lord's promise to those who trust in him is that he will *show them his salvation*. What is his salvation? His salvation is God himself. His salvation is Jesus. The name Jesus means "*Jehovah is salvation.*" It is in Jesus Christ that we truly come to know God and to know, in him, everlasting life. When God himself becomes our dwelling place, our place of refuge and shelter is the Lord Jesus Christ. It is there that we are promised life, eternal life, and salvation, in knowing the Lord Jesus Christ. He, my friend, truly is life. And in him, and through him, and because of him, we have this abiding promise:

Fear not!

PRAYER

Heavenly Father, we thank you and we praise you for being our dwelling place for all generations. You are our refuge and our fortress forever and ever. Thank you, Lord, that in our wilderness experiences, during our trials and challenges, you are our abiding place and our everlasting joy. In you, there is life and life to the fullest. And we thank you, Lord, that we have a place of safety, where fear cannot reign because Jesus reigns. We praise you that where Christ reigns, peace reigns. May your peace reign in our hearts because of the Prince of Peace, the one who wears Corona Victus, the crown of victory, rules and is Victor in our lives. We give you praise for this victory that overcomes the world, the victory of our faith in the One who is victorious—the Lord Jesus Christ, in whose name we pray.

Amen.

R.E.A.P. GUIDE

READ
- Psalm 91
- What lessons do you see the Holy Spirit teaching you in this text?

EXAMINE
- The main idea of this Psalm appears in verses 1-2. How would you express the main idea in your own words?
- What is revealed about God in verses 1-2, 4, and 9?
- Verses 3-10 describe the special protection of God's people. In what types of situations does God protect his people?
- Verses 8b and 10b describe a specific context for God's protection. What is that context?
- What is God's part in providing this protection (11-16)?
- What is the believer's part in receiving this protection (14-16)?

APPLY
- In what ways may we apply this Psalm to our situation with COVID-19?
- What are some ways this Psalm could be misapplied in our situation with COVID-19?
- What is revealed about our God that is always applicable?

PRAY
- Using the "PRAY" acronym, respond with **P**raise to the Lord, **R**epent of sins this Bible passage has revealed to you, **A**sk the Lord for any requests you have, and **Y**ield to his will.

ABOUT CLIMBING ANGEL PUBLISHING

Climbing Angel Publishing exists for the purpose of sharing stories of hope and encouragement, aiding in the gathering together of community, and supporting the process of betterment. The following books are available at most internet bookstores.

Adult Division: (Romans 8:28-30)

In His Image (English, Mandarin, & Romanian)
By Faith (English & Romanian)
My Birthday Gift to Jesus
Without Ceasing
SonLight
Art Bushing: His Diary, Letters, & Photographs of WWII (Volumes I & II)

Children Division: (Philippians 4:8)

The Christmas Tree Angel
The Unmade Moose
Thump
Somebunny To Love (English & Mandarin)

God does not want His children to simply *believe* in Him. He wants them to *experience* Him and know the sweetness of His loving provision.

SonLight is an inspirational tool for Christians to truly *experience* God on a daily basis.

Pastor Sam Polson leads you through the *New Testament, Psalms, and Proverbs,* all the while encouraging you with special antidotes and insightful wisdom, in a way that only a *seasoned pastor* can do!

ISBN: 978-1-64370-030-4

Learning to be a PRAYER WARRIOR is a JOURNEY.

Strengthen this ability in a group at your church with Dr. Dennis Davidson's book
WITHOUT CEASING!

Without Ceasing is available at a discount for small groups and church-wide initiatives.

Order direct from Climbing Angel Publishing by emailing:

ClimbingAngel Publishing@gmail.com

ISBN: 978-1-64370-033-5

Art Bushing:
His Diary, Letters, & Photographs of WWII

"As I read through this text, one word continually flashed through my mind: 'Amazing....' Indeed, here is a truly amazing book, on oh-so-many fronts!"
– *Sam Venable, author and Knoxville News Sentinel columnist*

"In short, these letters are windows into what it means to be human, in love, and dedicated to making the world a better place. May we all be inspired by them to find our own version of this experience."
– *Tom Bogart, 11th President, Maryville College*

Volume I, ISBN: 978-1-64370-027-4
Volume II, ISBN: 978-1-64370-028-1

www.ingramcontent.com/pod-product-compliance
Lightning Source LLC
Chambersburg PA
CBHW021110080526
44587CB00010B/458